Remembering Mom

By

Ellen Gable

FQ Publishing
Pakenham Ontario

Copyright 2020
Ellen Gable Hrkach
Published by
Full Quiver Publishing/Innate Productions
PO Box 244
Pakenham ON K0A2X0

Dedicated to the memory of
Betti May Gable Power
"Mom"
1934-2007

Mom and Me, May 22, 1982

Table of Contents

Introduction

"Death steals everything," wrote poet Jim Harrison, "except our stories."

My mother's stories didn't die with her. They live on in us: her children and grandchildren. That's why I decided years ago to write a book about her. Of course, finding time to do it has been a challenge.

Mom was a unique character. She endured many hardships in life but always tried to find humor in any situation. She wasn't a storyteller, per se, but she would often tell me anecdotes while we were in the car, shopping, or watching television.

There are so many things about Mom that I admired. But she was, after all, human with faults and failings like everyone else. And while she didn't attend college, I have always thought she was one of the smartest people I've ever known. When I was a child, I was amazed that she always knew the answer to every question I ever asked her. In that way, Mom was my hero. When faced with adversity, she was the strongest person I've ever known, and she always forged ahead, no matter what was going on.

On the one hand, she was generous to a fault, often going into debt when we were young so that my siblings and I could have plentiful presents under the Christmas tree. She bought theatre tickets for the religious sisters at my youngest sister's grammar school. She loved coming up to Canada and especially enjoyed surprising my boys with unexpected trips (and she never missed a Baptism or a First Communion or musical performance until she got sick). She had a unique sense of humor and was laugh-out-loud funny sometimes. Even today, she still makes me laugh. I'll remember one of her sayings, and I'll giggle out loud.

On the other hand, she smoked most of her life, could swear like a sailor, wasn't always faithful with church attendance, and would often yell from three rooms away. And…she was not the best person to keep a secret.

From the time I could remember, she worked from home typing court transcripts, so her housekeeping skills were only used during the spring and just before Christmas. Our house was usually messy and cluttered. But twice a year, it sparkled.

Mom could finish my sentences. Sometimes I could finish her sentences. Mom also had a knack for being able to pick out just the right gift at Christmas time. She knew what sort of clothes looked best on me and would often tell me, "Stop dressing like an old lady."

You can often tell the character of someone in their reactions to unexpected experiences, grief, or stress. I had never known Mom to be anything but determined and tenacious. She told me once that she was not originally the strong one in the marriage, that my father was. But that all changed after Dad's nervous breakdown. This came as a shock to me because I had always seen my father as the quieter, less assertive, parent. Mom had no choice but to be strong for her four small children and her husband, who sometimes could be like another child.

With this short book, I'd like to share my memories of my mom for the benefit of her grandchildren and especially for her great-grandchildren and future generations, who will never have the opportunity of meeting and getting to know this incredibly unique person in their family tree.

Sit back, relax, and enjoy these memories of my mother. I hope you will laugh, cry and maybe even feel inspired.

Ellen Gable Hrkach
May 2020

Chapter One
Beginnings

1936

Every human being has a beginning here on earth and an ending. My Catholic faith tells me that Mom's life didn't end; it just changed. I still talk to her (although admittedly, she doesn't respond, at least audibly!) I believe that Mom is in heaven, and I *will* see her one day when I enter eternal life.

In the summer of 2007, my mother was on hospice care with advanced chronic obstructive pulmonary disease (COPD) and approaching the end of her life. Since I live in Canada, I would make the ten-hour trek to my hometown in New Jersey every few weeks to help take care of her. During those times, we had many opportunities for discussion: about her life, her regrets, and about those things with which she was most proud. The one thing she wished she could take back was her habit of cigarette smoking. Even though she had quit years earlier, she knew that smoking was taking her from this life much sooner than it might otherwise have. However, she admitted that she had had a good life.

My mother was born Elizabeth Mary May on March 28, 1934, in Philadelphia, Pennsylvania. She was the fourth child and second living daughter of John and Elizabeth (née Gillespie) May of South Carlisle Street in Philadelphia.

Her older siblings at the time were Marie Florence (Aunt Flossie, born April 26, 1917, died September 22, 1988), John Frederick Jr. (Uncle Jack, born November 3, 1927, died August 3, 1997) and Edward (Uncle Ed, born April 27, 1929, died June 15, 1994). Three years later, Janet Teresa (Aunt Jan, born January 4, 1937) was born to complete their family. My grandparents lost a daughter named Dorothy about 1919, who was stillborn, although I can't find any birth or death certificates on Ancestry for this child. However, both Aunt Flossie and Mom told me about this baby and how grief-stricken and seriously ill with septicemia my grandmother was after this birth. I suppose this was the reason they waited eight years to have another child.

Mom's maternal grandparents were Amelia Veronica Ferguson Gillespie (b. 1874, d. 1953), whom she affectionately called Mom-Mom Gillespie, and John Joseph Gillespie (b 1866, d. 1920).

Her paternal grandparents were Laura Rabold, Mom-Mom May (b. 1877, d. 1948), and Frederick May, Pop-Pop May (b. 1873 d. 1951).

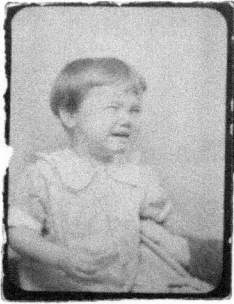

1936-37

When Mom was around three years old, Aunt Flossie took her to the photographer to get her picture taken. In most of the shots, Mom is crying. Aunt Floss brought Mom another time. Little Betty was a bit more cooperative, although she still wouldn't smile.

Early on, Mom was nicknamed "Betty." After she was married, she changed the spelling to "Betti." At the tender age of four, Mom was a junior drum major in her older brothers' drum and bugle corps.

L to R Mom's cousin, Joan, Jan, and Mom, circa 1939

Easter Sunday 1946

Mom was a feisty child, and at around age eleven or twelve, she played a practical joke on her sister, Jan (at the time nine years of age). She smeared Heinz ketchup on her head and on the radiator in the dining room of South Carlisle Street, then she lay next to the radiator and closed her eyes. When Jan came into the room, she screamed when she thought Mom was hurt. Then Mom opened her eyes and laughed. Jan yelled at her and was angry that she had played a trick on her because she thought Mom was hurt.

1947

Mom attended grade school at St. Richard's School on Pollack Street in South Philly and was crowned May Queen of the eighth-grade class in 1947. Being chosen as May Queen meant that you were the one who crowned the statue of Mary during the May Procession. (Twenty-four years later, my sister Diane was crowned May Queen at the same school.)

Grandparents

Mom adored her paternal grandfather, Fred May, whom she described as a kind, meek, and loving man. He made home-brew whiskey in his basement. Mom described him as not being "a drunk," but he did enjoy his whiskey. It was known throughout the family that Fred May was an American Indian. When Mom would ask her grandfather what kind of Indian, he'd just say, "civilized." Whether he was full-blooded or half, there's no confirmation of his heritage on Ancestry.

Fred and his wife, Laura, owned a music shop, but to make extra money, Laura opened her home to boarders. These boarders sometimes served as Laura's paramours. One day when Mom was about five years old, she watched as her beloved grandfather chased after one of the boarders (a man named Claude), pointing a pistol at the man. "Pop-Pop was the kindest, gentlest man I've ever known, but even Pop-Pop," Mom told me, "had a breaking point."

Mom also adored her maternal grandmother, Amelia Ferguson Gillespie, Mom-Mom Gillespie (Mom never knew her maternal grandfather, who died many years before she was born). Mom told me that Amelia was the kindest and most devout woman she had ever known.

However, there was one instance where Amelia wasn't so kind. When my grandparents (John and Bessie) got pregnant with Aunt Flossie before they

16

were married, Amelia kicked her daughter out of the house. "If you are grown up enough to do that, then you're grown up enough to find your own place to live." They eventually got married (in the rectory of the church, since John May, my grandfather, was a Lutheran). They had little money, so they moved into a friend's garage. Amelia eventually warmed up to the idea of their marriage and family. She lived with her daughter, son-in-law, and family (including Mom) during the last year or so of her life. (She died in 1953 from cancer of the liver).

Interestingly, my grandparents tried to keep that information secret, even celebrating their 50th anniversary in November 1965 (rather than in 1966, when they would have actually been married 50 years.) My grandmother would never have guessed that that information would be easily obtainable in the 21st century via Ancestry.com.

Mom was not particularly fond of her paternal grandmother, Laura May. (I based a character on her in my book, *Emily's Hope*. However, the book *is* fictionalized).

What is true is that Laura seemed to have more affection for her dogs than her grandchildren. One day when Mom was around ten, and Aunt Jan was around seven, Laura took them to the market. Mom told me that she was so excited she would finally be spending some time with her grandmother. And she and Aunt Jan were thrilled to be going to the market.

However, when they reached the market, Laura told them to wait inside the car until she returned. Needless to say, Mom and Aunt Jan were extremely disappointed that they didn't actually get to see the market or spend time with their grandmother. They never went on another day trip with her.

L to R: Amelia Ferguson Gillespie (Mom-Mom Gillespie), Elizabeth (Bessie) Gillespie May and John F. May (Mom's parents, my grandparents), and Fred May (Pop-Pop May).

This portrait was an anniversary present for my grandparents:
May siblings circa 1945 back row, Ed, Jack
Front row, Jan, Floss, Betty

Uncle Jack wasn't smiling because he had come in late the night before, and Aunt Flossie made him wake up early for this portrait.

Hallahan High School
Mom attended John W. Hallahan High School for Girls in Center City, Philadelphia. She loved her years at Hallahan and had many fond memories.

Prom Date
Mom went to the Christmas Prom (in 1950) with her cousin, Jack Friel (1931-2004).

Christmas Prom, December 26, 1950

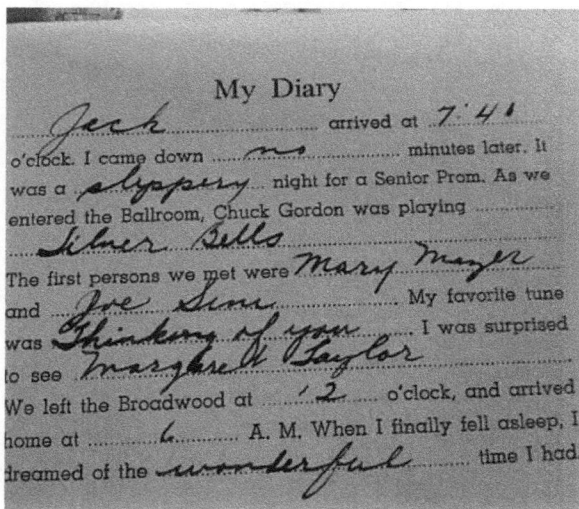

My Diary

Jack arrived at *7:41* o'clock. I came down *no* minutes later. It was a *slippery* night for a Senior Prom. As we entered the Ballroom, Chuck Gordon was playing *Silver Bells* The first persons we met were *Mary Mayer* and *Joe Sims* My favorite tune was *Thinking of you* I was surprised to see *Margaret Taylor* We left the Broadwood at *12* o'clock, and arrived home at *6* A. M. When I finally fell asleep, I dreamed of the *wonderful* time I had.

Mom's Prom Diary
(What was she doing until six a.m.?)

Mom was a proud graduate of Hallahan High School (Class of '51). She was also a proud alumnus and attended every Hallahan reunion (except for 1961, when she was pregnant with my brother, Frank.)

1951, age 17

1954

Blind Date

In early 1954, Mom was dating a man named Joe Nuzzi. She thought she loved him, but when he left to serve in the Army during the Korean War, an acquaintance asked Mom whether she wanted to go on a blind date with a man named Frank Gable. Mom was under the mistaken impression that "Frank" was tall because she had known of another Gable (Tom, Dad's younger brother, was over six feet tall). Mom stood five feet, six inches. Since Mom thought that "Frank" was also tall, she wore heels. When she showed up for the blind date, Mom was surprised to find her date was Frank (my father), not Tom, and Frank was much shorter than his brother. Mom said she was instantly attracted to my father, and after a few more dates (without the heels), she sent her boyfriend, Joe, a "Dear Joe" letter, which Joe later told her that he had "ripped up" because didn't want to lose her. However, Mom was already smitten with Dad, and they were engaged a short time later.

Wedding

January 15, 1955, dawned cold and frosty. Mid-morning, the white clouds appeared like they might let loose, but neither snow nor rain came. "I was so happy that day," Mom told me. "I was so much in love with your father."

They couldn't afford much, so they went to New York City for their honeymoon.

Mom wore flats, and during photos (like the one below), she bent her knees slightly so it would appear that she was shorter than my dad (she was a bit taller than he was).

January 15, 1955, L to R: Frank Gable Sr, Margaret Hamilton Gable, Dad, Mom, Bessie Gillespie May and John F May

Left to Right: Francis Carrelli, Ed May, Jack May, Tom Gable, Frank Gable (Dad), Betty May (Mom), John F. May (Pop-Pop) Janet May, Floss Gara, Peggy Gable, Janet Volpe

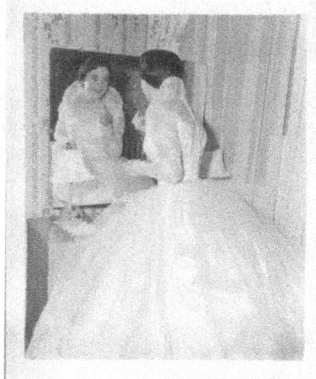

They moved into an apartment in Philadelphia. When they came home from their honeymoon, one of the first meals Mom made for Dad was spaghetti. However, when she was boiling the spaghetti, she mistakenly added too much salt to the water. My father gobbled up the spaghetti and never complained.

During this time, Mom explained later that, like most couples of the '50s, my father was the driving force in their marriage: he made most of the decisions and was the more assertive of the two.

Chapter Two

Becoming A Mom and Hard Times Ahead

I once asked Mom what the most memorable days of her life were, and she answered, "My wedding days and the births of my children."

My oldest brother, Michael Francis (Mike), was born on January 11, 1956. My sister, Diane Elizabeth (Di), was born the same year on December 24, 1956 (d. March 7, 2019). I followed a few years later (Ellen Donna, born May 5, 1959), then my youngest brother, Francis John (Frank) was born on May 30, 1961.

After giving birth to my oldest brother, Mike, Mom became pregnant again in June and gave birth to my sister, Diane, six weeks early, (weighing in at three pounds, fifteen ounces) on Christmas Eve, 1956. At her birth, the doctor said, "I can't believe it, two exemptions in one year!" (referring to the tax exemptions). Diane remained in the hospital until after the New Year. I'm sure it was difficult for Mom to care for two babies, and, in those days, the mother was the primary caregiver.

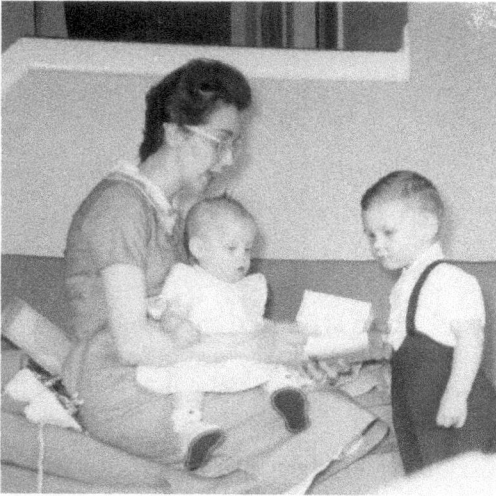

Mom with Di and Mike, 1958

The first house my parents bought was at 2407 Denfield Street (the living room of which is in the above photo) in a brand-new section of Camden, New Jersey called Fairview Manor. All the streets were named after World War II Army generals: Denfield, Patton, MacArthur, Wainwright et cetera.

My parents paid $9,800 for the house in August 1957, and our family lived there until 1969.

In the early years on Denfield Street, our closest neighbors were Bert and Tom Wilson and their children, Tom, Kathy, and Nancy.

Evidently, in September of 1958, Mom and Dad had a

frisky time on the living room floor, and I was conceived. (Yes, she actually shared that information with me!) When I came along in early May of 1959 (five weeks early), Mom said I just slid out of her (at four pounds, eleven ounces), and she hardly felt a thing. She called me a "good baby." According to Mom, I was a calm and quiet baby.

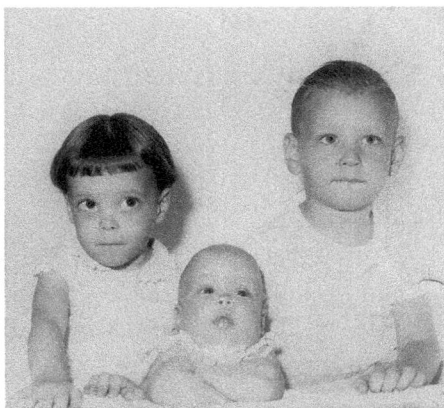

Diane, me, and Mike 1959

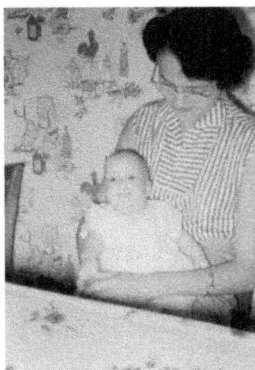

Mom and me, 1959

Less than two years later, Mom became pregnant with my youngest brother, Frank. At the end of her pregnancy, she was big and would grunt when she leaned down. She told me that I would mimic her and grunt just like her. Also, I heard my father and others calling her "Betti," so one day, when I was in the backyard, I knocked on the door and called, "Bay ee!"

It was also during that spring that my father was in the beginning stages of a mental breakdown.

Difficult Times, Ancora
I can't imagine what it must have been like to be nine months pregnant with your fourth child, and your husband in the middle of a psychotic breakdown. That is the situation that my mother found herself on May 29th, 1961. She woke up to find my father listening to the radio and telling her that God was speaking to him through the radio. He had no idea who he was or that he even had a wife and children. Dad picked up my sister, Di's, jump rope, and studied it like he was examining a science project. Mom escorted him to their bedroom and shut the door.

Mom *had* noticed signs earlier. He hadn't slept well in weeks. The previous Sunday, without warning, he walked five miles to Cooper Hospital, where she was scheduled to have their baby and was surprised and upset to find she wasn't there at all. He telephoned her from the hospital, and she told him to return home, convincing him it wasn't her time yet.

But Dad had never experienced full-blown psychosis before. In the years leading up to his nervous breakdown, Dad was still mourning the loss of his father (in 1959, just before I was born), as the two were remarkably close and worked together. What made the situation worse was that the new boss at his workplace treated Dad like he was a second-class citizen. Dad endured verbal abuse for the next two years before he finally quit. That, added to the emotional wounds he had suffered from sexual abuse by a priest when he was a teen, eventually led to his nervous breakdown on May 29, 1961.

Mom first called Aunt Flossie and, when she arrived, they went into the bedroom to check on Dad. He had taken all his clothes off and had started writing on himself with a ballpoint pen. She helped him get into a pair of jockey shorts but left him in the room, shut the door, and discussed with Aunt Floss the next plan of action and to check on the kids who were sitting in front of the TV in the living room.

It was at that point that Mom began having early contractions, but Aunt Flossie confirmed what Mom already knew: that my father would have to be committed to a psychiatric hospital (the nearest one was Ancora Psychiatric Hospital in Hammonton, NJ, twenty-five miles away). First, they had to convince him to go along willingly.

Mom then called Uncle John (Dad's uncle), and he

immediately came. He helped my father get dressed. Mom told Dad that they would be taking him to visit the doctor to "give him something that would help him sleep." He seemed agreeable to that, so he went with Uncle John and Aunt Floss, who escorted him out of the house, my mother following behind. On the way down the stairs, Dad picked up my sister's jump rope again and asked if he could take it, to which Mom and the others agreed that he could.

Mom had already begun having contractions and asked Aunt Peggy (Dad's younger sister) to come and stay with Mike, Di, and me (then ages five, four, and two).

The day after Dad was committed, Mom gave birth to my brother, Frank. It was Memorial Day (May 30). Mom had always wanted to name one of her sons after my father, but Dad had balked at the idea. My father had named Michael, Diane, and me. She figured that since Dad was unable to help name this baby, she would take the opportunity and name her youngest child after his father, Francis or Frank (he was nicknamed Frankie Boy).

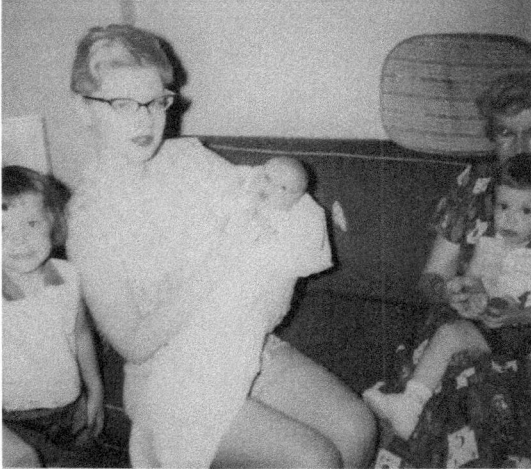

Just after Frank's birth, June 1961
L to R: Diane, Aunt Peggy holding Frankie,
Aunt Marie and me on Aunt Marie's lap

Every Sunday after that, Uncle John, Aunt Marie, Grandmom (Dad's Mom,) and Aunt Peggy would make the trek to visit Dad in Ancora. I was only two years old at the time, but I do remember snippets of those visits.

1961, Dad and Me at Ancora Hospital's Picnic Area

I remember one time sitting in the front seat on Aunt Peggy's lap (with no seatbelts). It must've been a warm day because I had fallen asleep, and when I woke up, Aunt Peggy's shirt and my hair were soaking wet.

Another memory I have of those visits to Ancora was seeing some of the people there and not entirely understanding why they didn't look "right."

I remember us driving away during one visit. I glanced back to see my father standing at a window staring at us. I couldn't see his face, but I remember feeling sad that we were leaving him again.

Since Mom had a new baby, three small children, and few skills, she needed to go on social assistance while Dad was in Ancora, and I know from later conversations that she hated — despised — being on welfare. She wanted to work for a wage. Aunt Floss and Uncle Dick, as well as Uncle John, all assisted financially.

There was one point when Dad returned home on a weekend leave. I don't remember much about it, but Mom told me that he accused her of cheating on him while he was gone (my mother remained faithful the entire marriage), so he had to be quickly taken back to Ancora before the weekend visit was over.

Dad Finally Returns Home

After much trial and error, which included electroshock therapy, the doctors at Ancora eventually discovered a treatment regimen that included several medications that kept my father's mental illness under control. It was just before Thanksgiving in 1961 that he finally came home.

My father returned home, but, according to my mother, he was a different person. Although my father was never an extrovert, before his nervous breakdown, my father had been the more dominant, in-charge spouse. My mother, who had previously been less of a take-charge kind of person, had to become the more assertive and even-keeled spouse.

To cope with what he had endured, my father began to write. Mom didn't encourage him because Dad wasn't the most eloquent writer, but I can understand how writing about his experiences was therapeutic for him. I'm thankful we still have some of his essays and the beginning of a novel he was writing.

In late 1961, Aunt Ele (Eleanor Eastman, Dad's older sister) moved into a home on the same street. She had just become a widow, and she and her daughters, Mary, Karen, and Linda, now lived across the street. During one incident, Aunt Ele was babysitting me at her house. When Aunt Ele took my hand to walk me across the street, I was so excited to see Mom that I let go of my aunt's hand and darted out into the street and was nearly hit by a car (according to my mother, that car screeched loud and long and came within an inch of striking me, although by some miracle it didn't.) My mother, already under the stress of dealing with my father's mental condition, four small children, and the fact that my dad couldn't find a job – and now nearly losing her precious, happy two-year-old toddler – grabbed me and slapped my legs so hard that Aunt Ele had to pull her off of me. As Mom explained to me years later, she loved me so much that the prospect of losing me was too much for her to bear. That, coupled with all the other stressful events going on in her life, brought her to the breaking point.

I certainly understand why she reacted that way. That incident must have gotten the message across in my little toddler mind that I should never go into the street, because I never went into the street again as a young child.

In retrospect, I don't remember the incident at all – which is surprising because I have a lot of memories from when I was two years old. But I do recall being afraid of stepping into the street when I was very young. I never understood this fear until Mom shared the story with me, and then it all came together and made sense.

In those days, spanking children was commonplace, and it was the only method of discipline most parents knew. When I mentioned it years later, Mom had become sensitive about it, knowing that it wasn't her finest hour.

For me, though, I completely understand why she reacted that way.

Early Memories of Mom
I remember being at the grocery store when I had just turned four years old. I was sitting in the front section of the shopping cart and sucking my thumb (which I did until I was twelve). A female acquaintance of Mom's stopped, and they chatted.

"Is this Ellen?"

"Yes," Mom replied.

"Is she two yet?"

"Two? She's four."

"Oh, my," the woman said, "she looks like a baby."

(Of course, I'm sure the thumb in the mouth didn't help.)

Much of my early years were spent in a playpen. The TV was usually on with programs like Chief Halftown, Pixanne, or Romper Room.

You Can Dress Her Up But...

Mom always took pride in dressing us up in fine clothes for different holidays. We always had new outfits for Easter and for Christmas. No matter how nice we looked, however, I usually found some way to mess up my hair or my dress. Mom used to call me a "good-natured slob." Proof below (I'm the one with the messy hair) and the one who can't sit like a lady.

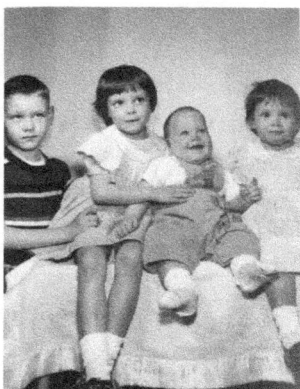

L to R: Mike, Diane, Frankie, and Me, 1962

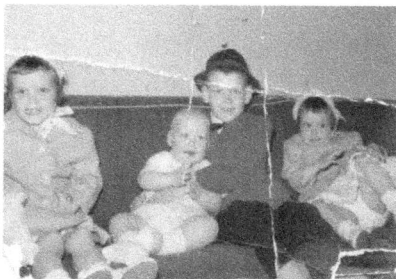

Easter 1962
L to R: Diane, Frankie, Mike, Me

Trips to the Shore

In the early '60s, we didn't own a car. So several times a summer, Uncle John would take the Eastmans and us in his station wagon for day trips to the Jersey shore at Margate. Usually, he'd bring Aunt Marie, his sister, along as well. I don't know exactly *how* they fit six kids, a baby, and four adults in the station wagon, but I do recall being in the back section on many of those rides (and, yes, with no seatbelts). These were fun times where we were always within walking distance to Lucy, the Elephant. Mom slathered us with baby oil to "protect" us from the sun. Mom and Aunt Ele packed a picnic lunch.

I don't have many specific memories of those trips, but I remember being in awe of Lucy the Elephant (although back then, it was in a state of disrepair and it smelled like urine).

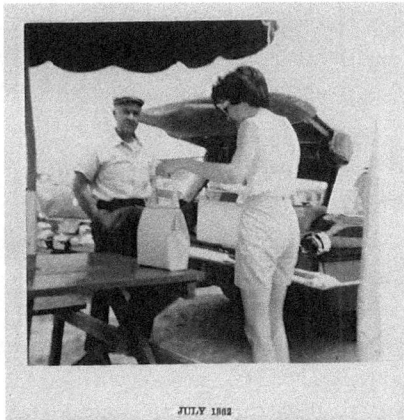

JULY 1962

Uncle John and Mom, July 1962 at the shore

39

At Margate with Lucy the Elephant, August 1962
L to R: Mom, Mary, Mike, Di, Ellen,
Aunt Marie (back), Karen (in front) and Aunt Ele

November 22, 1963

My parents adored President John F. Kennedy. He was Catholic, young, handsome, and charismatic. The Kennedys were like American royalty. My parents liked his wit and sense of humor.

When JFK was assassinated, I was only four years old. I don't remember much about that day other than my mother and father crying. That scared me because I had never seen them cry before (Mom had sheltered us from Dad's breakdown, for the most part). In the ensuing three days, the television remained on constantly. I remember being annoyed that nothing was on TV other than "news." And I can still remember the sound of those drums on the day of the funeral.

They bought a copy of the *Life* Magazine special edition on the assassination a few days later (which my brother Frank still has). Like most Americans, his death affected them for years to come.

They kept a framed photo of JFK in our living room until we moved to Philly in 1969 (that same framed photo currently resides in my storage room).

Transcriber Extraordinaire
In the two or three years after his mental breakdown, my father had a series of temporary jobs. Most employers were not interested in hiring a person recently released from Ancora. With her husband home but unemployed most of the time, Mom had no recourse but to try to find work from home. Uncle John and Aunt Floss continued to help financially. Eventually, Mom came off welfare and was finally able to find a job with a woman named Betty Proth typing envelopes for a penny per envelope and never again depended on social assistance.

Betty Proth became a friend of Mom's and invited us to her pool when I was about four. I remember that visit because I hung onto the side of the above-ground pool the entire time. Mom had coaxed me to jump into the pool. "You won't let me go under, will you, Mommy?" I asked.

"No, no," she said.

So I jumped into her arms, and she dunked me under the water. When I came up, she was laughing. "See, it wasn't so bad to go under the water?"

It wasn't so bad, but I was mad at her for dunking me. When I got out of the pool, I wouldn't go back in again.

In the mid-1960s, Mom eventually got a job transcribing court hearings for court reporters. The work paid much better and was more interesting. This was back in the day when she used carbon paper for copies. For every mistake she made, she had to erase several copies' worth. It was also back when she had an IBM Selectric typewriter. She typed so fast that it sounded like machine gunfire.

After a few temporary jobs, my father finally landed employment with the United States Post Office in Camden, New Jersey. His daily work shifts began early in the morning, so he went to bed by eight or nine p.m. (In fact, it was common knowledge that whenever Mom hosted late-night social gatherings for them, Dad was always comfortable going to bed, even while the guests were still partying.) He spent his days off sleeping most of the day.

When she started working more hours from home,

Mom would put me in front of the TV, and she enrolled Frank, my three-year-old brother, in nursery school. At the time, my brother, Mike, and sister, Di, attended the local Catholic parish school, Sacred Heart. That school did not have a kindergarten.

Sometime later, Mom bought me a lunch box for "school." I thought it sounded exciting to go to school until she finally brought me there (by bicycle, neither of us wearing helmets, with me on the handlebars, since we didn't own a car at the time). As we rode up to the school, Mom told me the name of the school was H.B. Wilson School.

When she started to hand me over to the teacher, I remember thinking that Mom was NOT going to leave me at this strange place! The teacher, a kind middle-aged woman, told my mom, "Don't worry. She'll be fine. Leave her with me." I thought, *I am NOT going to be fine.* As soon as Mom left, the teacher brought me inside, gave me toys to play with, and, as I became accustomed to the teacher and the classroom, I forgot that Mom had left me and had a fairly good first day. After that, I enjoyed attending kindergarten.

Messy House
Mom wasn't the tidiest housekeeper, but I never really cared about that sort of thing. As I was growing up, I can only remember feeling loved, wanted, and safe.

However, to say that our house was a mess most of the time would be an understatement. It usually looked like a hurricane swept through it. Two times a year (Spring and Christmas), Mom would go crazy and clean from the bottom up, vacuuming, scrubbing everything she could get her hands on. And while she cleaned, she played the record player at the highest volume (much, I'm sure, to the chagrin of our neighbors). She played "Fiddler on the Roof," "Greatest Hits of Motown," and "Man of La Mancha" (her tastes were very eclectic). I remember these times because I enjoyed helping her clean, and it always felt good to be in a spotless house for a few days.

Mom also liked to sing at the top of her lungs. She sometimes sang on key and sometimes not, but she was always funny. She would sing: "A Bushel and a Peck," (from *Guys and Dolls*) and belt out Carmen Miranda's "*Mamãe eu quero*" (which I always thought was Ma Ma Ma Ketto.) She could also sing a great rendition of "A Wandering Minstrel" from *The Mikado* (I didn't discover where that song came from until recently when my youngest son was watching a performance of *The Mikado* on YouTube!)

My siblings and I were accustomed to her unusual behavior, but when we had visitors, it was interesting to watch their reactions to her singing or playing the record player at full blast. I remember thinking, *Don't only kids blast their stereos?*

A Daily Nap

Mom had always been an early riser, but ever since I could remember, she also was a night owl. However, she took short naps every day, sometimes for just fifteen minutes. One day when I was about six years old, she was lying down on the couch and asked me to get her a blanket. I placed the blanket on her, then kissed her forehead (like she did for me when she put me to sleep). I'd never heard her laugh so loud.

Before she napped, she'd put a game show on TV, or a soap opera, then lie down on the couch. I once asked her why she had the TV on if she was going to sleep. She told me that that game shows and soap operas helped to put her to sleep (although she loved *The Price is Right)*.

She'd sometimes fall asleep for longer and start snoring, then wake herself up. She would've given us great material for social media if we had Facebook, YouTube, or TikTok back in the day.

Holiday Memories 60s

Holidays were special for Mom, but Christmas was Mom's favorite time of year. I think one of the reasons she wanted to make Christmas magical for us was because she didn't feel that it was all that magical when she was growing up. If she and her siblings were lucky, they each received an orange, a few pieces of candy and a small toy like a tiny ball or jacks for Christmas.

From the time I can remember, Mom would start shopping as soon as she received her Christmas Club check in October and finish well before Christmas. She loved baking cookies, especially a special recipe she got from our then next-door neighbor Ann Caprara called Raspberry Preserve Cookies (recipe included in the Appendix). She made these cookies (as well as butter cookies and chocolate chip cookies) every year right up to the Christmas before she died.

When she baked, she always let us lick the bowl or the beaters (I guess raw eggs didn't bother us back then.)

In particular, I will never forget Christmas of 1966 because it was magical for many reasons. A few days before Christmas, when we put up our tree, the four of us kids must have been misbehaving because Mom threatened us that Santa wouldn't come if we continued to misbehave. I still believed in Santa, and that worried me, so I made sure I was on my best behavior.

Well, Christmas morning arrived, and Santa *had* come! For a moment, though, we were all distracted by the sight of stark white outside. We had so much snow that we couldn't see our car parked in the driveway. We didn't always have a white Christmas, but this was a LOT of snow: everything was covered in beautiful shimmery snow.

Santa had brought bikes for every one of us. My other special gift was a Cheerful Tearful doll. Back in those days, my family would attend Mass on Christmas Day. As any normal kid would feel, I didn't like having to leave my toys to go to Mass, and this was one Christmas we didn't have to leave the house on Christmas Day.

Celebrating the holidays circa 1964
Clockwise from Aunt Flossie in the back, Mom, Dad, Frankie,
Mike, me, Diane, Mom-Mom and Pop-Pop.
Uncle Dick was taking the picture.

Another annual tradition took place on New Year's Eve when Mom would make her grandparents' Vegetable Soup recipe in a large stockpot (recipe in the Appendix). She would then stick the pot outside in the cold weather overnight, then warm it up the next day. We'd watch the Mummers Parade on TV, and anyone who came to visit got a piping hot bowl of vegetable soup. No matter how many people visited, we always had enough to be put into the freezer for later enjoyment.

Learning to Drive

It was around this time that Mom learned how to drive. Until that point, it wasn't all that necessary because we didn't own a car. But Mom wanted to learn how to drive because she knew eventually that she and Dad would buy a car. Uncle John taught Mom how to drive. From what she told me, he was a patient teacher. That doesn't surprise me since he was a naturally patient man.

The Halloween Princess Dress Fiasco

When I was in first grade, I got the part of the princess in the Halloween play. Mom bought me a princess costume; it was puffy, blue, and shimmery, with a wand I could hold. Mom told me to make sure that I didn't get it messed up because we still had to go trick-or-treating that evening. So I went off to school in my beautiful blue princess dress, performed in the play. Afterward, there were refreshments. I don't remember whether I knocked

48

into someone or what, but grape juice spilled down the front of my beautiful princess dress. When I got home, all Mom could say was, "El!" Of course, there was no way to remove the purple stain from the beautiful blue dress, so I went out trick-or-treating as a sloppy princess with a stained dress.

Hot Summer Night

Although I was toilet-trained by the age of two, I didn't quite master going all night without wetting the bed until I was 14. Mom was always very patient about it, although my sister Diane wasn't too thrilled about sharing a bed with me. Mom eventually bought me my own bed.

One hot summer's night around 1966, my father told us to all bring our bedclothes down to the living room where we had a small window air conditioner. I was especially excited because it felt like we were having a slumber party. Of course, I wasn't thinking about the fact that I would not be dry in the morning. In the middle of the night, amidst my sleeping parents and siblings, I woke up feeling wet and sticky. I went up to the bathroom, turned the light on, and then noticed in horror that what covered the lower half of my body wasn't urine. That's when I smelled what was all over my pajamas. I started crying for Mom, and she immediately came up the stairs and tried to console me. I must've smelled awful, and I'm sure she would've rather been sleeping than cleaning me up. But the gentle way she washed me and dressed me in dry clothes made me feel like she didn't mind at all. In later years, when Mom was sick, and I helped to clean her after she used the bedpan, she would keep saying 'thank you' over and over again. I reminded her of that incident, and I said, "You've done so much for me that if I can give back to you just a tiny bit of what you've done for me, I'm happy to do this for you." (That made her cry.)

Health Problems and Weight Loss
Throughout most of her life, Mom was a chain smoker (from the age of thirteen) and a daily consumer of Pepsi. She smoked and drank Pepsi as she sat at her IBM Selectric typewriter, transcribing trials and depositions.

Eventually, she was diagnosed with kidney stones and spent over a month in the hospital. I remember visiting her on Easter Sunday of 1967 (children weren't allowed to visit in hospitals back then). My father arranged with one of the nurses on duty to secretly bring my sister, brothers, and me in to see her. When they wheeled her into the small hallway, I almost didn't recognize her. My brother Mike (eleven years old) thought it was cool that he could wrap his fingers around Mom's wrist. There was something else different about her, though. She seemed to barely smile when she saw us. The visit lasted for maybe ten minutes. Mom, still weak from kidney surgery and weight loss, finally abruptly cut the reunion short. Mom told me later that she had remembered that visit because she barely had enough strength to keep her eyes open, let alone visit with us kids.

While she was in the hospital, Dad and Aunt Floss encouraged us to write letters to Mom. My brother, Mike, wrote a letter in which he listed every state and its capital. I'm sure Mom had a good chuckle at that. Neither Mike nor I know where that letter ended up. I wrote two letters, and I remember writing each of these letters.

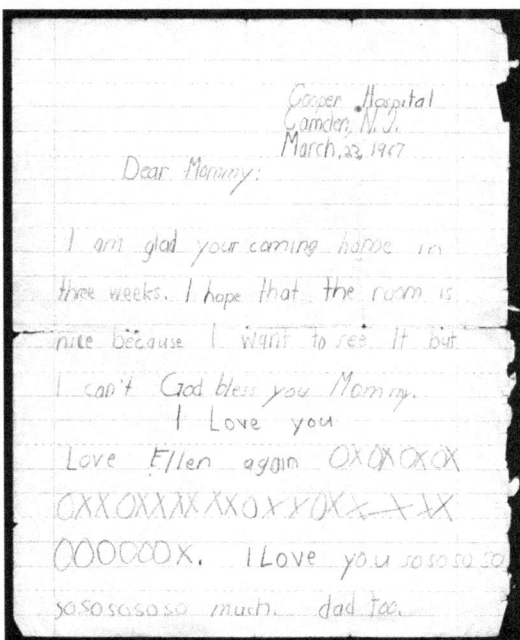

One of the letters I wrote to Mom
when she was in the hospital

One night when my mother was still in the hospital, I woke up to the sound of someone crying. I snuck out of my bedroom and into the little hallway of our house on Denfield Street. The hallway led to a landing overlooking the living room. My father was sitting in a chair, his head in his hands, and sobbing and muttering. "What am I going to do if I lose her? I can't lose her. I can't lose her." I wanted to go down the steps and tell him everything would be all right, but I felt like I shouldn't disturb him, so I returned to my bed. As I did every day, I prayed for Mom to get better. I didn't realize how serious it was and never even considered she wouldn't get better.

Eventually, the doctors removed her damaged kidney, leaving her with one kidney, and she finally began to get better. They recommended that she drink lots of water every day (until the day she died, she always had a glass of water nearby).

When I consider how sick Mom was and how she recovered, I'm confident that God heard my father's prayers and everyone's prayers for her recovery. Later, Mom told me that the doctors didn't expect her to survive.

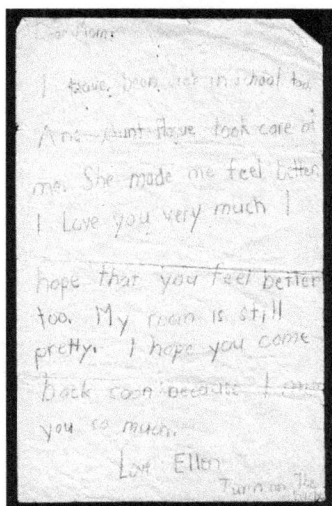

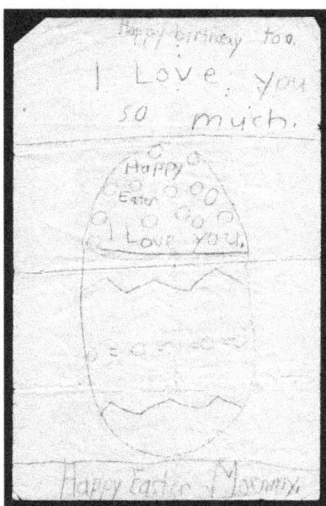

Another letter I wrote to Mom while she was in the hospital

Back then, most people had little, if any, comprehensive health insurance. Because of that, at the end of Mom's stay, she was presented with a hospital bill for $1,618.30. (In today's dollars, that would be about $12,640). Thankfully, the hospital allowed her to pay $5 per month to pay off the bill. When she started working outside the home in the mid-'70s, she paid $10, and then $20, per month and finally paid the hospital bill off just before James and I got married in 1982.

After that hospital visit, she never had another serious health problem again, until she got chronic obstructive pulmonary disease (COPD) later in life.

And instead of a glass of Pepsi at her desk, while she typed, she always had a glass of water there.

Page one of the three-page Cooper Hospital Bill for Mom's lengthy hospital stay in March, April 1967

Mom was already thin when she became sick (about 105 lbs), but she lost a great deal of weight while in the hospital. She was about 80 pounds when she was released. As I recall it now, she looked a lot like the photos of the people in the concentration camps after the war, a walking skeleton. Since she had lost so much weight, the doctors encouraged her to eat an ice cream sundae with lots of whipped cream every day so she could put on weight.

Over the next year or so, Mom dutifully followed the doctors' advice to eat an ice cream sundae every day, and she slowly, but surely, began gaining weight.

Whenever the Mr. Softee truck came around, she would order an ice cream sundae for herself and cones for us (and sometimes a cone for our dog, Chalkie). Within weeks, she was back to transcribing again. It was good to have her home. It took years for her to gain back all the weight she had lost, so eventually, she stopped eating ice cream every day (but still indulged every now and then).

Falsies and Frankenstein Scar
Even before Mom's surgery, I remember one time when I was about six or seven going into her bedroom and watching her stuff rubber things into her bra.

"Why do you put those things in there?" I asked.

"You mean these?" She showed me one. It was pink and rubbery with a nipple on it.
I nodded.

"It's a falsie."

"A what?"

"A falsie. Women put them in their bras to make them look bigger up top."

"Oh." I didn't say anything else, but I always wondered why she felt she needed to use those.

Not too long after Mom's surgery, she showed me

her scar. It went from her belly button right around her stomach to her back and looked like a red railroad track. It was still fresh and purple-red when I first saw it, and it scared me.

"Looks like a Frankenstein scar, doesn't it?" Mom asked.

I nodded. "Does it hurt?"

"Not anymore."

"Really?"

"Really."

As I got a bit older, if I had to use the toilet while she was getting out of the shower, I'd see the scar again and would be reminded of how long and how horrible it looked. By the time I was a teenager, the scar had faded and was just part of who Mom was, but it still looked like a Frankenstein scar.

The Second Time I Saw Mom Cry
In the summer of 1967, Mom-Mom (Bessie Gillespie May) had a stroke and a heart attack. She was in critical condition and couldn't speak. She died just after midnight on July 23 that year. The next morning, we were all getting ready for Mass when I heard the sound of Mom crying in the living room. At this stage, it was only the second time I saw her cry (the first was when JFK was assassinated). I can

still picture her clearly in my head: she was dressed for church, sitting on the couch in our living room at Denfield Street, and was crying and blowing her nose with her handkerchief. In between sobs, she said, "I can't believe she's gone," and "she couldn't even ask for a drink of water." I remember patting her hand and telling her that everything would be all right. I didn't like seeing Mom sad because it made me sad too. I loved my grandmother, and I was sad that she "had gone to heaven." But I was still quite young and couldn't grasp the enormity of Mom's grief.

A New Pair of Glasses

One day in school towards the end of winter in early 1968, my third-grade teacher, Sister Rita Clare, handed me a note to bring to my mom. I don't remember whether I read the note, but when I brought it to Mom, she said we'd have to take a trip into Philly to the eye doctor.

We went the following week. It was fun taking a day off from school to go into Philly. I especially enjoyed having Mom all to myself. We had a car, but Dad used it for work, so we took the F Bus to get to Dr. Gottlieb's office in Center City Philly. Dr. Gottlieb, a tall, middle-aged man, loved children, and he made the eye exam fun. I picked out a new pair of glasses, and Mom made an appointment for two weeks later when the glasses would be ready. As we were leaving, Dr. Gottlieb leaned down close to me, pointed to his cheek, and asked me to give him a kiss, which I did readily. It might be considered creepy nowadays, but back then, it wasn't.

In all this time, I hadn't realized that to watch television, I basically had to sit with my nose on top of the TV screen. My vision had gradually become worse, so I never noticed.

When Mom brought me back to the eye doctor's office, Dr. Gottlieb sat me in the high examining chair and brought out my glasses.

"Look how pretty they are," he said. They were light blue and pointy on the ends. I thought these glasses were the most beautiful thing I'd ever seen. But when he put them on my face and adjusted them, my mouth fell open, and for a moment, I couldn't speak. Everything in the room became crystal clear. Colors were brighter, people actually looked like people, and it seemed like the greatest moment of my young life. Both Mom and Dr. Gottlieb were laughing as I kept pointing out things I could see clearly.

As Mom and I walked the streets of Center City, I kept pointing out words on the signs in the store and on the street. "Look, Mommy, it says 'Lit Brothers.'" We stopped at Horn and Hardart's for lunch (I always ordered chicken and rice with gravy because Mom never cooked rice at home, and I loved rice). As I was eating my lunch, I kept telling her what time it was because I could see the big clock on the wall of the restaurant. I talked constantly like that the entire walk to the bus stop and the trip home. I was probably a nuisance, but Mom was very patient with me, smiling and laughing every time I told her I could see something.

New glasses

A Changed Neighborhood
In the mid-1960s, an African American couple moved in a few doors down from us. Mom and Dad had always taught us to treat every person as we would want to be treated. And when that one black family moved in, just about everyone else's house posted a "for sale" sign the next week. Within two years, the neighborhood went from being all white to 85% African American. My father, God bless him, initially was firm. He was determined to show our new neighbors that we were not like those other people who put their houses up for sale. We would remain with them in the neighborhood, no matter what. Both my parents, I think, prided themselves on bringing us up to ignore the color of a person's skin and to see only a fellow human being.

Our next-door neighbors became good friends of our

family: Pearl and Bill Shines were a middle-aged black couple with a friendly German Shepard named Galvin. At the time, I would have been around eight or nine years old and about the size of a four-year-old. I loved Bill's personality and his stories so much that I used to greet him by jumping up on him, and he would pick me up and throw me in the air then hold onto me. I remember him saying things like, "I wish I could bottle her energy." One day, he came into our living room while I was crying, and he picked me up and sang, "Big girls don't cry," in a high voice like Frankie Valli, which made me stop crying because Bill sounded funny when he sang. Another time, he picked me up and remarked to Mom, "She sure is color blind." Mom replied, "Yes, she is." I remember thinking, *I'm not color blind!! I can see colors!*

A Lasting 'New to Us' Car

Before the mid-1960s, my parents owned one or two cars, but the cars were used (and cheap), so the vehicles didn't last long. Around 1968, my parents bought a gently-used, light blue Rambler (with financial help from Uncle Dick and Aunt Flossie).

Now that we had a reliable car, I became Mom's driving companion, usually in the front seat. Wherever Mom went, she'd always ask if I wanted to come along. We went everywhere together: bowling, grocery shopping at the Acme or Shop Rite, clothes shopping at Korvette's or J.C. Penney's in Audubon. I remember one time when we were driving to

Korvette's, a woman cut in front of Mom, and Mom called out, "You P*$%%." I never swore, but I said, "No, Mom, that was a C*%@." Mom laughed so hard, probably at my high-pitched voice using that vulgar term.

I remember having a lot of conversations with Mom on those short car trips, telling her what was happening in school, or asking her questions about things. As I said previously, Mom always seemed to have an answer to any question I asked. For example, when I was in the process of telling her what the highest mountain in the world was, she interrupted me and said, "Everest." She didn't have a college degree, but she was one of the smartest people I've ever known.

Our shopping trips together continued right up until I got married in 1982 and moved to Canada. Even when I returned home for visits, Mom would say, "Come on, El, let's go to Sam's," or "Let's go to Acme," or "Let's go to the fruit stand."

Voting: Every Citizen's Duty
In early November of 1968, I had just had minor surgery, so I was home from school. It was election day, and Mom took me to the nearby Morgan Village Middle School, where she went to vote. On the way there, she told me how important it was to vote. Of course, I'd always asked, "Why?" She'd always say the same thing: "Because it's our duty." I believe Mom voted in every municipal, state, and federal election from the time she was 21 until her death.

First Lesson in the Facts of Life

Back in those days, people didn't generally spay or neuter their pets. Just after Thanksgiving in 1968, our dog Chalkie became pregnant. We had had this sometimes-snappy black-and-white mongrel for three years. A few times a year, she would go into heat. I didn't know what being "in heat" meant, but I knew when our dog was going through it. One night, while Chalkie was in heat, she was in the backyard. Out of the blue, we heard yelping coming from the yard. Mom and I and my siblings ran out to the yard. Chalkie and another dog were stuck together. Mom stood there, not knowing what to do. Our neighbor, Bill, said, "I know what to do," then he tossed a bucket of water onto them, and that pulled them apart. The whole thing was very strange to me. I thought Chalkie was hurt, so why was she jumping around like she was happy?

Just after the New Year began, Mom told us that Chalkie would be having puppies in the next month or so.

I remember thinking that it was the best news ever since I naively thought we would be keeping all the puppies. Aunt Floss asked Mom, "Are you going to let the kids watch when the puppies are born?" Mom didn't miss a beat. "You bet. There's no better way to learn about the miracle of life than watching a dog have puppies. It'll be the best lesson in the birds and the bees." I remember asking myself what we could learn about birds and bees from watching puppies be born. Anyway, by the time Chalkie went into labor on a cold, early February afternoon, Mom made sure that the dog was in a comfortable cardboard box with a blanket and took her to the basement. We all sat down by the box and watched. We asked a lot of questions. "Where did the puppies come from? How are they getting out? Why is she licking them down there?"

It seemed like it was over in a few hours. Chalkie had given birth to four puppies, and I thought they were the cutest things in the whole world. The next day, when we woke up to get ready for school, Mom surprised us by saying, "There's another puppy! Chalkie had one more during the night!" When Mom first went down and saw the fifth puppy, she thought it might be dead. But he was alive. Mom seemed more excited than we were. Of course, we were thrilled, and we all peeked at this new puppy before we left for school.

Every day I'd come home from school and rush down to see the puppies. My favorite was the only female of the group who looked like the twin of her mother. I was quickly becoming attached, and Mom surely noticed. She warned me. "El, you know we can't keep the puppies, right?"

This didn't help prepare me or my brothers and sister when the puppies were finally old enough to go. Dad had them all in a cardboard box, and they were yelping. Tears were surely flowing because all of us kids wanted to keep at least one. "Please, can't we just keep one? Can we keep the girl puppy?

Please?"

I don't remember who decided, whether it was Mom or Dad, but Dad finally took the girl puppy from the box and handed her to us. We gained a new puppy, and her name was Tinker.

I remember that Diane named Chalkie, but I don't recall who gave Tinker her name. And, yes, we were all thrilled!

A Broken Heart

The Christmas before the puppies were born, Mom and I visited Pop-Pop (John F. May) at his South Philly row home. I remember being so happy because it was Christmas day, and I had just received a doll. I brought the doll with me to show my grandfather. I also wanted him to open the gifts we brought him. On our way over the Walt Whitman Bridge, Christmas songs were playing on the car radio, and I'm sure I had a perpetual smile on my face and in my heart.

When we knocked on the door, I could hear Pop-Pop's voice telling us to come in. He sat in his chair by the door and was leaning forward, his head in his hands. He didn't look up. We greeted him with "Merry Christmas," but he didn't respond. I stood by his chair while Mom put his food on the table. He sat straight up and stared ahead. A cigarette burned in an ashtray nearby, and Pop-Pop took a puff of it every few minutes. What little hair he had was not combed, and he had scruff on his cheeks and chin. My cheeriness dampened. I nudged Mom's sleeve and held up a bag of gifts we brought for him. She took the bag to show him. "Dad, we've got some gifts for you to open."

He shrugged his shoulders and pointed to the coffee table. "Put 'em over there." His living room had no tree or decorations. It was messy, and Pop-Pop said, "Your mother would be rolling over in her grave if she saw the place now."

Mom tried to cheer her father up, but Christmas or no Christmas, he was in no mood to be cheered up. I wanted to show him my doll, but I didn't think he would be interested. When we left, Mom said, "Pop-Pop doesn't have a will to live anymore, not since Mom-Mom died." Mom explained that Pop-Pop loved Mom-Mom so much that his heart was breaking. As we drove home, I felt sad for him and prayed for him.

I tried to remember better times with Pop-Pop. He used to put me on his leg and make a clicking sound as he lifted me up and down like I was on a horse.

Six weeks later, around the time the puppies were born, my grandfather died. Mom wasn't surprised. She was sad but told me later that she knew it was coming, and she was happy that he was with Mom-Mom.

His death left his row home in South Philly (the

house my mother grew up in) vacant.

The Bowling Alley
One of the things Mom enjoyed was participating in a bowling league at the nearby bowling alley. Mom was an excellent bowler. There were a few years when she belonged to more than one league. The one she belonged to the longest was called the Rainbow League. Most memories I have are of going to Camden Lanes, which was close to our house on Denfield Street. She also later bowled at Baker Lanes in Cherry Hill, NJ.

Mom bowled several games at near-perfect (280 or above). Our next-door neighbor, Bert Wilson, also bowled with Mom. Her other bowling friends were Marge, Fran, and Snooky. I used to accompany Mom and hang out with Bert's daughter, Nancy, at the bowling alley. Even when we moved to Philly, Mom continued to bowl at Camden Lanes.

Later, when I was about fourteen, Mom encouraged me to start using makeup. She showed me how to apply eye shadow, mascara, and lipstick. One night, before Mom and I went to the bowling alley, I put on blue eye shadow and a bit of mascara. Mom told me I looked much older with makeup. Besides, I *wanted* to look older.

At the bowling alley, my friend, Nancy, and I went to the cafeteria for a snack. I walked up to the counter and said, "I'd like some fries and a Coke." The middle-aged lady turned to another lady and said, "Get a load of the little girl with the makeup." The two women had a nice chuckle. That was the last time I wore makeup for a few years.

Chapter Three
South Philly

The Move to South Philly

In 1969, we still lived in Camden. However, after a young girl was sexually assaulted in broad daylight a few doors down from us, my parents felt they didn't have any choice but to put our house up for sale. I didn't want to move because I had many friends of all different races.

In the summer of 1969, we sold our house (for $11,600), moved to South Philly, and lived in my maternal grandparents' house on South Carlisle Street for two and a half years. My parents needed time to save money for a down payment for another home in Jersey. We knew that we wouldn't stay in Philly for long.

On the corner of 15th and Pollack Streets was a deli, and behind the counter worked a heavyset woman named Ann. She wore her hair pulled tightly back in a greasy ponytail and usually had a cigarette with an extended ash hanging out of her mouth.

One day that first autumn, Mom sent me to the corner deli to buy her an ice cream sundae. (It had been two years since Mom's surgery, but she was still very thin). As usual, Ann made the sundae. I noticed the ash from her cigarette getting longer and longer until it dropped into my mom's sundae just before Ann put the whipped cream on top. My mouth fell open, and I'm sure my eyes were wide. I said nothing, took the sundae home, and explained to Mom that she shouldn't eat it because the ash from Ann's cigarette went into her ice cream. Mom threw it out and never sent me there again.

Mom also used to send my brother Frank to Ann's Deli. One time she sent him there for her usual sundae, and Mom waited, but he never returned. So she walked up to the deli and found Frank playing the pinball machine with the change from the sundae, now melted. He says, "She forthwith yanked me out of there by my ear." Needless to say, she didn't send him for an ice cream sundae again.

The Facts of Life (Part 2)
In the house in South Philly, Mom almost never closed the bathroom door when she had to go to the toilet. The reason I remember that so distinctly is because it was there, while she sat on the toilet, that she told me "the facts of life." I had just turned eleven years old; it was the summer before I attended sixth grade. I happened to pass the bathroom upstairs on Carlisle Street, and she told me about someone who had just a baby. I innocently asked how the baby got in there. I wasn't really prepared for the answer, but she told me in such a nonchalant

fashion that it made me less uncomfortable. Then she reminded me of when Chalkie got pregnant and had her puppies and how they came out of her. But I was shaking my head for days because I just couldn't believe a married couple did things like that. Animals, sure, but not people.

A few weeks after that, we were visiting Aunt Flossie's house in Northeast Philly, and on the TV that day was a documentary on PBS showing an actual (and non-medicated) vaginal birth from the point of view of the doctor delivering the baby. Admittedly, I was enthralled. Giving birth looked like it hurt...a lot! But I couldn't pull my eyes away from the television. I had always wanted children, but after seeing that, I wasn't so sure anymore.

A New Job for Ellen
Later that year, Mom asked me if I wanted a part-time job, a 'real' job, working for someone else. There was no hesitation. I said yes. Mom was instrumental in getting me a job at Saint Richard's Rectory, about four blocks from our house on South Carlisle Street. I worked with two other girls, and we filed the empty church envelopes according to the number of their house and the street. It was a big parish in those days, so it took a lot of time. I worked after school every day for two hours, and I made two dollars a week (in those days, an enormous sum for an eleven-year-old). Mom knew I was a saver, so I saved the two dollars a week until Christmas, then I bought Christmas gifts for everyone with the money.

Chapter Four
Sudden Loss, New Love

On New Year's Eve in 1971, my parents attended a party at a parish hall in Runnemede, New Jersey. I had heard of Runnemede before because Mom's aunt (Mom-Mom's younger sister, Regina or Jean, for short) and cousins Joan Davis and Kathleen Olsen lived there. It was at that party that someone mentioned that their house was for sale, so my parents went to see the house sometime after. Within a few weeks, Mom told us we would be moving to Runnemede on Holy Thursday of the following year.

New Year's Eve 1971

I didn't want to leave my part-time job at the parish rectory, but I also realized that this was what Mom and Dad had been saving up to do.

Until that time, we had all attended Catholic schools, but when we moved to Runnemede, Mom enrolled us all in the public schools because it was free. They were low on funds since buying the house and could no longer afford the Catholic school tuition.

One of the things I loved to do in this new neighborhood was to ride my banana-seat bicycle (in those days, no one wore protective helmets). I hadn't been able to ride far in South Philly because of traffic, but in Runnemede, I was able to ride wherever I wanted. One day, a little neighborhood girl asked if I would take her for a bike ride. (Although she was only six and I was thirteen, she was bigger than me.) We went up Center Avenue, then down Third Avenue, with her on the back of my bike. Well, what I didn't realize was that Third Avenue was steeper than it looked. The little girl's extra weight, and the speed I was going made for a dangerous combination. My bike skidded and crashed against the sidewalk. The little girl, who was now crying, got a small scrape on her knee, but I had a long and large, burn-type abrasion (road rash) along my outer thigh. It was perhaps the biggest scrape I had ever seen and was starting to bleed. When I came home and showed Mom, she immediately took me by the arm to the bathroom to put on the Merthiolate (the orange stuff that stung like the dickens). As she was pulling me, I was resisting, but I was no match for her: me at four feet tall and her at five feet six inches tall. I'm sure I screamed loudly enough for the entire neighborhood to hear. After she dabbed the orange stuff on my very painful abrasion, she then said, "There. You're done. That wasn't so bad."

"Yes, it was," I countered.

Overnight, that rather large abrasion made me sick to my stomach and dizzy. In the morning, I told Mom I was too sick to go to school. Besides, my pants kept sticking to the wound. After a day or so, I returned to school with a note from my mother.

I stood over her shoulder as she typed the note. Initially, she wrote: "Please excuse Ellen for her absence. She was sick because of a boo-boo." When she typed the words 'boo-boo,' she turned, eyebrows raised, and smirked at me.

"Mom, you can't write that. A boo-boo?" At the time, I didn't know how to define my injury, but I learned that it was called an abrasion. Mom retyped the note.

More Lessons in the Birds and the Bees
Since Chalkie had never been spayed, it was only a matter of time before she got pregnant with more pups. It happened again in 1973. This time, Chalkie gave birth in a cardboard box in my parents' room with Tinker looking on anxiously. Tinker had also never been spayed, but for some reason, she never

got pregnant in all the years we had her.

Once the pups were old enough, Mom settled them and Chalkie in the basement. This was where things got strange with Tinker. She started to nurse some of the pups and began lactating. I remember Mom calling all her friends with this remarkable story of a dog who'd never been pregnant but was nursing puppies. Mom was right. We had all become more educated in the birds and the bees. However, this time, we were in our teens, and Mom warned us that we would not be keeping any of the pups.

Another thing I remember about our dogs is that around this time, my parents started feeding them liver. They cooked it every night, and I used to get nauseated just smelling it. I'm not sure why they gave them liver instead of dog food. I seem to recall perhaps one of the dogs was low in iron.

Christmas, 1975
Mom on the chair (whoever was taking the photo
cut Mom out of the photo!) with Tinker
on her lap and Chalkie in front.
Mom was their favorite human!

My Trip to France
From the time I was a freshman in high school, I dreamed of traveling to France on a school trip that was scheduled for my junior year. Mom told me to save every penny of my birthday money and Christmas money. I did, but six months before the school trip, I only had about $100 saved up. I needed $500 more (a lot of money in those days). "Why don't you ask Aunt Flossie?"

I suspect Mom had already talked to Aunt Flossie to make sure she would say yes. But at the time, I wouldn't have known this. So I wrote down what I wanted to say and called. Mom stood next to me. I asked Aunt Floss if she would lend me the money for the trip to France. "Of course, Tootsie Roll! (That's a name she called most of her nieces.)

My trip to France was a trip of a lifetime, and I enjoyed it very much. I was so grateful to Mom for suggesting that I ask Aunt Flossie and thankful to Aunt Flossie because I was able to go. When I returned home, I got a job at Roy Rogers Restaurant and paid back Aunt Flossie about ten dollars a month. When I had to give that job up to start shadowing for a court reporting career, I asked Aunt Floss if she would give me a few months before I started paying her again. At that time, I think I owed her about $150, but I had misplaced the paper that had the correct amount. Once I got a job in the court reporting field, I called her to ask her how much I still owed her and to tell her I would be starting payments again. Aunt Flossie's response was, "You know what, El? You don't owe me any more money."

"Yes, I do, Aunt Floss. I'm sure I still owe you over $100."

"No, you don't. That's my gift to you. You don't have to pay any more."

"Really? Thank you so much, Aunt Floss."

In some ways, Aunt Floss and Mom were two peas in a pod. Both were generous to a fault.

A New Dog
After Chalkie died in October of 1976, we were all so sad, that Mom decided we'd get another dog. A week after Chalkie died, Mom and I visited the local pound and picked out a rambunctious mongrel puppy we named Sugar (I think Mom came up with that name). Sugar came by her name naturally because she loved food, eventually gained a lot of weight, and was diagnosed with diabetes (the irony escaped no one). I remember Mom going out to the backyard in the morning to collect Sugar's urine and test it. That was the epitome of Mom's love of dogs.

Sugar and Me, 1976

Working in Philly

During the mid- to late '70s, Mom started working outside the home at the District Courthouse at Eighth and Market Streets in Philly. During a big trial, it was common for the lawyers to want the transcripts immediately (this was called 'daily copy.') There were usually two or three court reporters working, so that after one reporter spent an hour or so in the courtroom, another would take his or her place. The original reporter would dictate his notes into a machine called a Dictaphone, and my mother, or the other transcribers, would then listen to, and type it.

She enjoyed working in downtown Philly. Even though I was in high school, I missed her being at home full-time and our outings together. By the time she returned home, I was usually in bed, so I couldn't tell her about my day at school. Eventually, once she got used to working crazy hours, she started going shopping on the weekends and, of course, would ask if I wanted to go along. Even as a teenager, I didn't like the fact that Mom was working outside the home, but at least we had weekends that we could go to the store together.

Coping With an Alcoholic
When I was younger, I remember Dad getting drunk a few times, but I don't recall him becoming a full-blown alcoholic until I was a teenager. After his gall bladder surgery, one of his doctors suggested that he drink more beer to calm himself, although Mom thought that was the stupidest advice she'd ever heard.

Those three years that my father was an alcoholic were sad and uncomfortable. Dad eventually joined Alcoholics Anonymous and then spent a year or so on the wagon, then a few months off the wagon. When Dad was off the wagon, he walked around in his underwear in a drunken stupor. Then he'd stop drinking for some time and then start drinking again. It went like that until April of 1978. He used to proudly say, "El, I haven't had a drink in (so many) days." And, like most self-centered teenagers, I'd say, "Great, Dad," pat him on the back and walk away without thinking much about it.

April 22, 1978
Despite the fact that Dad had fallen off the wagon again, Mom was determined that we would go ahead with a trip we had planned to Akron, Ohio.

We had already planned a trip to visit Dad's

youngest sister, Aunt Peggy, but Mom specifically scheduled it during the Pro-Bowlers' Tournament of Champions, which happened to be in Akron that year.

Mom had gone on a similar trip with my cousin Linda the previous year, and they had had such a good time, that I begged to go the next year. Of course, we would watch the pro-bowlers' tournament, but Aunt Peggy had many other activities planned. She and Uncle Frank and their son Chris lived in a gigantic home with many rooms. I remember telling Aunt Peggy, "I hope someday I have a house this big when I get married, but I want to fill all the bedrooms with kids." Aunt Peggy chuckled. "Better you than me, kid."

The first few days of our trip were exciting and memorable. We visited malls, watched the pro-bowlers' tournament, and went out to dinner. We played board games (Aunt Peggy and Uncle Frank were extremely competitive, I soon found out!) For the upcoming Saturday, Aunt Peggy had bought tickets to a dinner show to see *Tony Bennett Live.* Saturday morning, I was planning for another exciting day when the phone rang. My brothers were on the phone. They were distressed that my father – who had been in an alcoholic stupor – had taken a bunch of pills and collapsed, and they couldn't wake him. Mom was concerned, but she tried to remain level-headed and told my brothers to call the ambulance. An hour or so later, from upstairs at Aunt Peggy's house, I heard my mother screaming and saying, "God, no!" In that split second, with the news that my father was dead, our lives changed forever.

Our trip came to an abrupt halt. Uncle Frank took Mom and me to the airport to return home to New Jersey. At the ticket counter, the service rep, a young man, gave my mom a hard time about the fact that we were not using the tickets we had already bought. "These tickets are non-refundable," he said, straight-faced and ignoring that Mom had told him that her husband had just died. Mom was doing everything she could to keep it together and not burst out crying.

Uncle Frank (God bless him) started swearing at the man. "Are you f-ing kidding me? This woman just lost her husband, for (blank's) sake. Get someone the (f…) out here who can help them get home. And if I have to pay for her (blank) damn ticket home, I will." Well, the man behind the counter turned white and went – presumedly – to get someone who could help us.

Back in those days, airplanes had smoking and non-smoking sections. When they asked if we wanted non-smoking or smoking, Mom, her eyes glassy, said, "El, do you mind if we sit in the smoking section? I need to smoke." I agreed because I didn't have the heart to say no.

The whole thing seemed like a nightmare. Just as the plane took off, Mom began to cry. I was also on the verge of tears, but I felt like Mom needed a shoulder to cry on, so I stayed strong and held in my emotions. She sobbed, talked, blew her nose, puffed on her cigarette, and cried more. She cried the entire time we were on the plane. I can't remember everything she said, but she kept repeating how much she loved him, despite all the problems he had had, despite his mental illness and his alcoholism.

When we arrived home, our house was filled to the brim with relatives who had come to pay their respects and sympathies. The sight of everyone, sadness etched in their faces, was all I needed. I saw my cousin, Jan, and I burst into tears and couldn't stop crying. It was so overwhelming for me to lose my father, and I was upset that I hadn't been there when he had died. In looking back, I can't imagine how difficult it must've been for Mom to be away the moment her husband died.

The viewing and funeral were a blur, but I do remember Aunt Flossie helped to organize the clean up of the house because, in those days, that's where people congregated after the funeral Mass and cemetery. My sister, Diane, and her then-boyfriend, Jim, came home (from Chicago) to attend the funeral.

Since Dad was only forty-nine years old, and since most of us were still living at home, it was an enormous funeral with many of my friends, their parents, and my siblings' friends and parents attending. We had a huge extended family of aunts, uncles, and cousins who also attended. Dad was well-liked in the community and at the post office where he worked. Mom, my brothers, Mike and Frank, and sister Diane greeted hundreds of people who turned out to offer their condolences.

I recall seeing my father's first cousin, Joe Power, at the viewing when he came to pay his respects. Our family was closer to Joe's sister, Mary Sasso (whom we called Aunt Mary) since she and her family lived nearby in Glendora. All I knew about Joe at the time was that he was divorced and worked at the Philadelphia Navy Yard. Dad's mother (Margaret, my grandmother) and Joe's mother (Lizzie) were sisters. As cousins living in the same neighborhood, my father and Joe grew up together.

At the funeral Mass, the priest said that as Catholics, if we believe in heaven and eternal life, we will eventually see our father again. Jim, Di's boyfriend, said that statement had resonated with him. For me, it was comforting to know that I would eventually see Dad again. Little did I know it would be sooner than I expected.

Mom hadn't slept alone in twenty-three years, except for the times when Dad was in Ancora. So she asked me if I would sleep with her in their double bed in the weeks and months after Dad died to keep her company. I hadn't slept with someone in many years, so it was awkward. Most nights, as I was falling asleep, Mom talked to me and shared things about my father. I don't specifically recall what she said, but I felt uncomfortable that my mother was telling me personal things about Dad. However, I knew she needed someone to talk to, so I listened.

In those few weeks after he died, I had many dreams about Dad, dreams where he would say, "It was all a hoax. I didn't really die. See? I'm fine." And then I'd wake up, my snoring mother beside me.

Voracious Reader
When Mom wasn't typing, watching television, or talking on the phone, she was usually reading. I think one of the reasons I love to read is because she read so much. If a movie came out that was based on a book, she would usually try to read the book first. *The Exorcist, Jaws, The Boys From Brazil*, and *The Shining* were some of the books she read before she saw the movie. She enjoyed murder mysteries and, as I got older, introduced me to books by Mary Higgins Clark, Nelson DeMille, and James Peterson. (For more about her favorite movies, see the Appendix.)

New Loves
Mom was known for her ability to be direct and blunt. So later that year, my mother asked my Aunt Mary Sasso (she was actually my father's first cousin) if her brother (Joe Power) was "dating anyone." In other words, my mother was asking Aunt Mary to set her up on a date with her brother. Eventually, Joe called and asked Mom if she wanted to go to the Navy Yard's Christmas party.

On the one hand, it was beautiful to see Mom so happy and giddy again. Whenever she spoke of Joe, her high-pitched voice and wide grin said that she was "in love."

On the other, it was strange seeing her in a relationship with another man. At the time, some people thought that she was dating too soon after my father died. But that didn't bother me. What was strange was that she was acting like a teenager, and I wasn't used to that.

She looked forward to dates with Joe. They went to dinner and the movies frequently.

During this time, I had traveled to Canada and met my future husband, James. When I flew to Canada for my first visit there, I had a great trip. On my way home, I missed a connecting flight, and the airline put me up in a beautiful Montreal hotel. Back in those days, there were no cell phones, so I couldn't call Mom to tell her that I wouldn't be on the flight. As she told me later, she waited at the gate until every last person got off. Then she asked the customer rep at the gate if anyone was still on the plane, to which the girl replied, "No." Of course, Mom, with her wit, countered with, "Are you sure? My daughter is very short. You could've missed her," or words to that effect. Mom wasn't a worrier, and when I was finally able to call her from the hotel, she said she figured that I must have missed a connection.

I told her my flight number for the next morning.

After a year of flights visiting Canada three times, James finally flew down to New Jersey to meet my family on Easter weekend in 1980. Up until then, Mom had only talked to James on the phone, so this would be the first time meeting James.

His flight was scheduled to arrive at 9:53 a.m. Now, if you knew Mom, you'd know that she didn't care about being precisely on time, and sometimes she could be a tiny bit late (an attitude that both my sister, Laurie, and my husband, James, share). Mom *usually* wasn't late; most of the time, she was right on time. I, on the other hand, would rather be an hour early than a minute late.

So that morning, I was up bright and early and nagged Mom to leave for the airport by 9:10 a.m. (it only took fifteen minutes to get to the Philadelphia Airport from where we lived in South Jersey). She hemmed and hawed, and then we finally left at 9:35.

Well, wouldn't you know it? There was an accident and traffic was backed up, so we didn't arrive at the airport until 10:15 a.m. I was mad that we didn't leave earlier, but as soon as we parked the car, I ran to the gate where his flight was scheduled to arrive. When I looked at the screen to find out when the flight arrived, it had been EARLY and had already arrived at 9:47 a.m. When I got to the gate, James was not there. I had expected that he would wait at the gate for us, but unbeknownst to me, his mother had called her brother-in-law and his wife (who lived near the Philly airport) to meet James when his flight arrived.

When Mom caught up with me, I was nearly in tears. Of course, she was pragmatic about the whole thing. "Where would he go? It's not like he left the airport, El."

She suggested we go down to baggage claim, and there he was. I ran up to him and hugged him so tightly. Behind him were his Uncle Mike and Aunt Kitty. James introduced his aunt and uncle, and I introduced Mom. We finally got to the car and returned to Runnemede.

Once home, I proceeded to introduce James to the family (whoever was home at the time: Mike, Frank, and Joe, I think), then we went to the den, where we cuddled and spent time with each other. A day later, Mom asked to speak to me privately. Leaving James in the den, I went into the living room with her.

"So, El, are we ever going to have an opportunity to spend some time with this young man you think you might marry?"

It was then that I realized that I had been hogging James all to myself. So we spent the rest of that Easter weekend dividing ourselves between being alone and spending time with family (and attending Mass).

Around this time, my sister, Diane, had broken up with her long-time boyfriend, Jim, and she moved back home.

Second Wedding
Mom and Joe dated for about two years before they married in early 1981. It was a cool, overcast day, and the entire family celebrated their nuptials.

Most people found it interesting that Joe was my father's first cousin (Joe's mother and my father's mother were sisters). But Mom would always say, "I like to keep my husbands in the same family."

When asked which husband she would be buried with, she laughed and replied, "Whichever one I'm married to the longest."

She and Joe were married for 26 years before Mom died. She and my father were married for 23 years, so she was buried with Joe. (My sister, Diane, who passed away in 2019, was eventually buried with my father.)

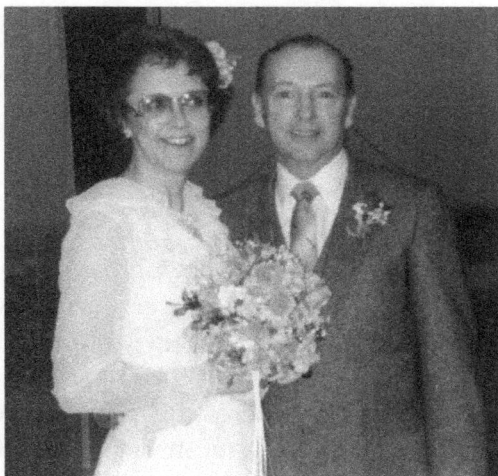

Mom and Joe on their wedding day, early 1981

Mom and Joe, cartoon by James Hrkach 1981

Chapter Five
"Take Two" and a Wedding

In early 1981, Mom called me into her bedroom. She had a wide smile on her face, and she pointed. I stared at her dresser, which was usually cluttered. At that time, the clutter had been pushed to the side, and a strange contraption stood in the center. It was a clear plastic rectangular container with a tube in the center and a little mirror showing a dark brown circle. She said, "Look!"

I had no idea what the contraption was. "What's this?"

"It's a pregnancy test."

"A what? A pregnancy test?"

"Yes," she was grinning from ear to ear.

"And I suppose you wouldn't be showing me if you weren't pregnant."

"That's right. I'm pregnant."

Admittedly, at the time, I was slightly annoyed, not that she was pregnant but that she was pregnant when I was engaged to be married, and preparing to move to Canada, and would not be around for much of the baby's life. For years before this, I had always begged my mom for a younger sibling, to no avail.

Eventually, I realized it wasn't all about me. I was thrilled that there would be another sibling in our family. It was hard not to be excited when Mom and Joe were so happy about the impending birth. It didn't seem to matter to them that they were both in their late forties.

Thankfully, Mom and Joe were both open to life. Although the pregnancy was unplanned, Mom never called their baby an accident. Instead, she called the baby a "surprise from God."

Mom's first visit to her obstetrician did not go well at all. When she informed the doctor (and he happened to be the doctor who delivered me twenty-two years previous), he said, "Just what do you plan to do with *it*?"

"What do you mean?" Mom asked.

"You can't have *it*. You have a one in ten chance of having a baby with Down Syndrome." He then went on to list all the possible abnormalities the baby could have and urged her to "terminate." "Besides," the doctor said, "you're too old."

"I'm having this baby."

"Then you'll have to get another doctor," he said.

I don't know what happened next, but I can envision Mom giving him a piece of her mind (and a few choice swear words). I'm sure she couldn't get out of there quickly enough.

She eventually found a pro-life doctor, and I'm sure she caused that fellow a few gray hairs because the pregnancy had complications given Mom's age and the fact that Mom continued to smoke.

When Mom and I went shopping while she was pregnant, I was surprised how often people would stare at her. Yes, she looked her age, and yes, she was pregnant, but did they have to stare so rudely? It bothered me more than it bothered Mom. She didn't seem to care who was staring at her. And, honestly, I had never seen my mother so happy.

I remember the day of my youngest sister's birth like it was yesterday. It was a rainy Tuesday, and Mom had been induced earlier that day. After a day of work, my three siblings and I finally made it to the hospital (Our Lady of Lourdes in Camden, New Jersey). Within a half-hour of arriving, we heard the cries of a baby beyond the closed doors of the labor and delivery unit. Then we saw a nurse wheeling out a baby. We asked whose baby it was. The nurse studied the card and said, "Tower."

"Wait! Do you mean Power???" We asked.

"Oh, yes, that's right. Power."

Finally, we were going to find out whether we had a new brother or sister. "What is it?" I asked.

"It's a girl."

"Yay! We have a new sister."   Laurie Elizabeth Power was born on September 15, 1981.

Joe came out to the waiting room and told us about our new little sister. Then he brought us into Mom's room. I was shocked at how good Mom looked, sitting up in bed with a happy smile on her face. The woman in the bed beside her was close to thirty years younger – perhaps a teenager – and her hair was messed up and sweaty, her complexion pale: obviously, she had been to hell and back. So why did Mom (thirty years older) look so chipper? I found out later that she had had an epidural (which she didn't have with any of us older kids). Joe didn't want her to have an epidural, so when he left the labor room to get something to eat, she asked the nurses to give her one because she was in pain. I don't think my stepdad ever knew that she had had an epidural!

Interestingly, some people have called Laurie my 'half-sister.' However, since my stepfather and my father were first-cousins, she's actually my three-quarters sister because we share three-quarters of our family tree (not one-half!). I've never really called her anything but my sister, though.

Laurie's Baptism 1981
L to R: Mom, Aunt Flossie (godmother)
holding Laurie, Joe

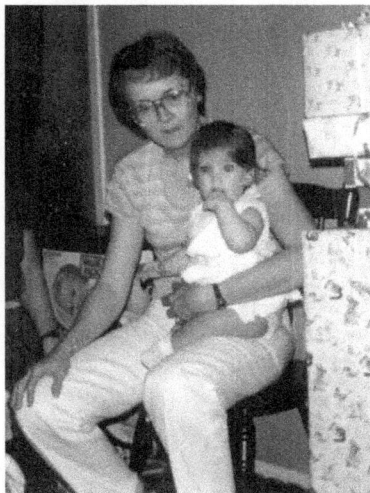

Mom and Laurie early 1982

Mom was a new mother again, and she and Joe enjoyed raising her: nursery school, dance recitals, school functions, everything that came with bringing up another child. Mom often shared with me that she felt "old" compared to some of the other mothers (many of whom were in their twenties and thirties.) But Mom especially enjoyed being a lunch mother at St. Teresa's School.

During the first eight months of Laurie's life, I was excitedly planning a wedding.

I was sad, though, that my father wasn't alive to walk me down the aisle or to dance "Daddy's Little Girl," with me. I think my father would have loved James, and it was bittersweet that I was getting married but without my father walking me down the aisle.

At that time, not too many mothers were walking their daughters down the aisle. So when I asked Mom to do it, she said she'd think about it. After a while, she came back with an idea: she would walk me down the aisle *if* Joe could also walk me down the aisle. At the time, I had only really known Joe for three years, so I was a bit uncomfortable about having him walk me down the aisle. But I wanted to please Mom, and I wanted her to walk me down the aisle, so I said yes.

In retrospect, perhaps some people thought it was strange that Joe and Mom walked me down the aisle, but I was happy because Mom was happy.

The day after the wedding, after packing everything for the move across the border and to Canada, James and I came back inside the house, and we said a tearful goodbye. Mom held Laurie, just eight months old, her big eyes wide open, just staring down at me, then looking at Mom, her head tilting, somewhat concerned. Mom sobbed, almost as hard as when my father died.

May 22, 1982,
L to R Shirley Hrkach, Mom, me, James, Joe, and Tony Hrkach

L to R: Betti, Flossie, Jack, Jan, August 1985

Mom remained close to three of her siblings, Aunt Floss, Uncle Jack, and Aunt Jan. Her brother, Ed, did not live close by, so she rarely saw him.

Aunt Flossie spent most holidays at Mom's place, sleeping on the trundle bed in Laurie's room. When James and I visited for Thanksgiving or Christmas, Aunt Floss was always there.

Mom always teased Aunt Floss because when she dressed for bed, it was usually with several layers of clothing and a warm, thick pair of socks, even when it was warm out.

The Shore

Every summer in the '80s, Mom, Joe, Laurie, and Aunt Flossie would spend a few weeks down at the shore in Wildwood. They often took Mandi (Di's daughter, Mom's first grandchild) with them. They rented the house from Dick Boyle, another of Joe's and Dad's cousins.

Mom and Laurie at the shore, 1983

At the shore with Mandi and Laurie, 1986

At the shore

Chapter Six

Special Memories and Sad Events

By the late '80s, long-distance calling was much cheaper, so Mom and I spoke every other day. At the time, I was the mother of two small children and finding the days so full. A few years later, I gave birth to another son and became even busier. One day, I felt overwhelmingly thankful to my mother for giving me life and for taking care of me for so many years. I sat down and wrote her a letter to thank her for being open to life and for bringing me into the world and for taking care of me. She kept this letter in her pocketbook for many years, and I found it in her drawer when she died.

I visited New Jersey at least three times a year, and Mom also tried to visit Canada once or twice a year (one of her visits was usually the week after Easter). She loved surprising the boys with her visits and seeing the shock on their faces when she drove up.

Grandparenthood

Mom enjoyed being a grandmother, although she could be very 'in your face' about parenting methods. But she could also be very respectful, saying, "They're *your* kids, and I'll be damned if anyone should tell you how to raise *your* kids." I don't think she agreed with our method of attachment parenting: not letting our babies cry it out, extended breastfeeding and the family bed. But she said she'd defend our right to raise our boys the way we thought best.

With Amanda (Mandi), her first grandchild, and my sister Diane's daughter, Mom took Mandi (only one year younger than Laurie) with her whenever she took Laurie somewhere.

When I was pregnant with my first son, Josh, I knew about the baby shower because, like Mom, my mother-in-law couldn't keep secrets. When I walked into James' Aunt Bonnie's house in Rhoddy's Bay for the shower, it was almost anti-climatic because no one shouted surprise. The women were just milling about. It didn't seem like anyone knew I was even there. I remember thinking, "What kind of strange shower is this?" Then I thought, *I wish my mom were here.* And lo and behold, there she was. It went from anti-climactic to joyful because Mom had come! She, along with Aunt Floss, my cousin Karen, my sister Laurie, and niece Mandi, traveled up to Canada and surprised me. That was the first time I realized that Mom *could*, in fact, keep secrets!

When I gave birth to Joshua, then to Benjamin, she said, "Did you use the Bible to find those names?" Then at one point, she asked, "What's the next boy's name going to be, Zachariah?"

At that time in her life, she and Joe were a bit more financially stable. She spoiled her grandchildren with every sort of material gift she could find. Birthdays and Christmases were filled with finding her grandchildren just the right gift, but she also bought them things they needed. And she always tried to come up here for the Baptism of any new baby we had.

Aunt Flossie's Death
Mom called me in the summer of 1988 to tell me that Aunt Flossie had cancer and that she would be having surgery. Mom was on the verge of tears. Aunt Floss had never smoked and was always extremely healthy. Initially, I wasn't too concerned because Aunt Floss was only seventy years old but looked much younger. I had expected her to live to a ripe old age of 100.

The plan was to remove any cancer with surgery and start Aunt Floss on chemotherapy and radiation. But when the surgeon opened her up, the cancer was everywhere, so he closed her back up again. She didn't have much time left. Mom adored her eldest sister because Aunt Floss had always been like a second mother to her. Aunt Floss eventually was put on hospice care and stayed with Mom until she was close to the end.

I came down for a visit just after Aunt Floss had her surgery. She knew she was dying and told me that she wanted me to have the scrapbook of all the notes and cards that she and her late husband (Uncle Dick) had exchanged over their twenty-year-long courtship and marriage. I told her I would be honored to keep that for her (and I still have it). She also asked me if I wanted to have her engagement ring/wedding ring set from her marriage to Uncle Dick, which I gladly accepted.

When she died in September 1988, everyone was sad. I remember Aunt Floss telling Mom and Aunt Jan to make sure that everyone at the luncheon after the funeral "had a drink" on her. At the end of the luncheon, drinks were purchased, and everyone made a toast to this remarkable lady. I still miss her.

Aunt Floss left her house and assets to Mom, Aunt Jan, and Uncle Jack. She also left money to Uncle Ed.

Just after Aunt Flossie died, James and I found the perfect house in our small town. However, we didn't have enough money for the down payment. When I asked Mom if she would lend me the money for the down payment, she said, (in the spirit of Aunt Floss), "Yes."

I paid Mom back a little bit each month. When I had paid back most of it, money became tight, and I asked Mom if she would mind if I skipped a few months. She said, "Of course." After about six months, we became less financially strapped, and I told her we were going to start paying it again. But she said (in the spirit of Aunt Flossie,) "You don't owe me any more money."

"But, Mom, I didn't pay back the entire amount yet."

"Yes, you did."

Well, I *had* kept track, and I knew there was still a quarter of what I had borrowed that I hadn't paid back. But Mom wouldn't allow me to pay any more on this debt.

Timmy's Baptism July 1992
L to R: Karen, Frank, Mom, Joe (behind her), me, Josh (in front), James holding Timmy, Mandi, Laurie holding Ben, and Diane

Smoking and Emphysema

Back in the late '70s, the doctor had urged Mom to give up smoking because her lungs had already begun to show signs of emphysema, even though she was only in her early forties. But as much as Mom tried, she couldn't stop. When she was about sixty-one (1995), the thought of Laurie growing up without her made her more serious about giving up smoking.

The doctor prescribed a nicotine patch for her, and she was finally able to stop. Although the damage had already been done, she was able to extend her life by quitting when she did.

The Only Time I Saw Mom Drunk
In the 1980s and '90s, Mom used to drink a Bud Light before bed. But I don't ever remember her getting drunk until 1995. Mom had planned a huge party (with open bar) for Laurie's eighth-grade graduation in June of that year. Mom was a social drinker (Bud Light or JB and water), but I never saw her drunk until that day. For some reason, I think the bartender just kept handing her a drink, and she kept drinking it. At the end of the night, she tipped the bartender an exorbitant amount. I don't think my stepfather was happy about that tip!

Ice Storm 1998
Mom didn't have the opportunity to see my kids very often: March break, summer, and Thanksgiving. A few times, we traveled to New Jersey during the Christmas holidays (although it was difficult, given the challenges of driving through upstate NY in a blizzard). She also talked to my boys over the phone, but it wasn't the same as being with them.

In early 1998, Ontario experienced an ice storm, and we lost all power. At the time, we didn't have a wood stove, so it was too cold to stay in our home. We packed up clothes and took our four boys to stay with my mother-in-law. At the time, I was homeschooling our boys (back in the days when it wasn't as popular as it has been during the recent pandemic).

Unfortunately, my mother-in-law was a clean freak, living in an exceedingly small condo. We later learned she had OCD (in retrospect, it made a lot of sense), so after a few days at my mother-in-law's place, I called Mom, nearly in tears, because I just couldn't spend another day there. We didn't know when our electricity would return since the ice storm had done so much damage. And, at my mother-in-law's place, my kids made a lot of mess, and I just couldn't clean up the messes quickly enough.

Mom came up with an idea to have James drive us to Great Bend, Pennsylvania, to meet with Mom, then Mom would drive us to New Jersey. James could then drive back to Canada. This way, James could make the trip there and back in one day.

I packed up more clothes and the homeschooling books for our kids to spend an extended visit with their grandmother. At the time, Josh was ten, Ben was eight, Tim was five and a half, and Adam was almost two.

Now, Mom had always wanted to forge a closer bond to Adam, my youngest at that time. Adam resembled Mom when he was a toddler, but he hadn't warmed up as quickly to her as the other boys because he had never been able to spend enough time with her. She would always say, "Gimme a kiss," in a strange accent to Adam. And he would respond very emphatically, "No!!" Or if I was nursing him, Mom would say, "I want some!" and he'd reply, "No!"

This time during the Ice Storm of 1998, we were at my mother's house for two weeks. We got to celebrate Adam's second birthday during this time. Mom bought him a Little Tykes basketball stand and ball. Mom had always sent us birthday and Christmas gifts, but she rarely was up in Canada to see the boys open up their gifts. The excited expression on Adam's face and his wide smile made Mom so happy.

During those two weeks, Adam grew particularly fond of his grandmother. When she asked for a kiss, he would gladly give it to her and hugged her and allowed her to read books to him. After a week or so, Mom exclaimed, "That ice storm was the best thing that ever happened because Adam finally knows me!!" After that, Adam was always happy to see his grandmother.

Mom and Adam 1996

Chapter Seven
Near Miss and Medical Setback

In the spring of 1999, Mom and Laurie came up to Canada for a visit. I was nearly nine months pregnant with my youngest son, Paul, and I couldn't drive because I was so big that I had to pull the seat back so that my stomach wouldn't press hard against the wheel. Then my foot couldn't reach the pedal. So Mom drove us wherever we needed to go. At the time, my husband James was rehearsing for *Fiddler on the Roof*, so Mom had the idea to pick up two homemade pies at the local small-town bakery. The plan was to give one to James and the rest of the cast at the rehearsal, and we'd keep one for our after-supper dessert. On our way to the rehearsal, after picking up the pies, Mom was driving. All of a sudden, a car pulled out onto the road without looking. Mom slammed the brakes, and we narrowly missed the car and skidded into the other lane. As we skidded, Mom threw her right arm out across my big belly to protect the baby. Thankfully, no one was coming in the opposite direction, or we would've been in bad shape. Our car finally stopped, and Mom asked if I was okay. I told her I was fine, but that I was sure my heart had stopped for a moment. The elderly man got out of his car, and Mom went to speak with him. I'm not sure what

Mom said to the fellow, but it looked like Mom downplayed it. When she got back into the car, she said, "He said he was sorry that he didn't look both ways, but I think he's too old to drive. He had to be in his nineties." She sighed. "His mistake could've killed us."

Mom glanced at the back seat of the car. The two pies were mangled and on the floor. She picked them up and, with her usual wit, said, "Well, it's a good thing that these are the only casualties!"

Paul arrived on time and safely, thanks to
Mom's quick reaction and excellent driving.
Paul's Baptism, June 1999
L to R: Back: Karen, Mom, Frank, Josh, Laurie,
Me holding Paul, and James
Front: Karli, Ben, Thomas, Adam, and Timmy

A New Job and Pneumonia

In the late nineties and early 2000s, Mom worked as a court recorder at the local traffic court in Runnemede. She turned the tape recorder on and kept track of which case was heard at which time. During our every-other-day phone calls, Mom would always tell me about the most interesting cases. She seemed to enjoy the work.

In early 2004, the family had just started making plans for a surprise 70th birthday party for Mom (who would turn 70 on March 28 that year). The invitations were sent, the restaurant was reserved, and we were all excitedly looking forward to surprising Mom.

As it turned out, this new occupation as a court recorder at the local traffic court in Runnemede was also where she picked up a bad case of pneumonia. When doctors tell people to stay home when they are sick, they mean it. For someone like Mom, who already had pre-existing conditions and breathing problems, catching that particularly virulent strain of pneumonia made her extremely sick.

The day before she became critically ill, I had called Mom while I exercised on the treadmill. I loved talking to her— especially when I was exercising – because it made the time pass quickly. However, this time, my stepfather told me that she wasn't feeling well. He handed the phone to her, and all she said was, "I feel lousy, El. Like I have the flu or something. I'll talk to you later. Love you."

The next morning, I got a call from my sister-in-law, Karen, who said Mom had taken a turn for the worse. Joe had called the ambulance, and Mom was now on a ventilator in the intensive care unit. She was diagnosed with pneumonia, and the prognosis was not good. The nurses had told her to tell any relatives who lived far away to come immediately, as she wasn't expected to live much longer. Of course, I remembered another time when she wasn't expected to live, but that had been thirty-six years before, and she was much younger.

I gathered up my boys (I was still homeschooling three of my five sons), packed our bags, and my husband drove to Great Bend, Pennsylvania, and my brother, Frank, picked us up. While my sister-in-law, Karen, watched over the kids, my stepfather, sisters, and brothers kept vigil. Mom, who had been given Ativan, a strong narcotic sleep aid, remained unconscious for over a week, even when the doctor discontinued the Ativan. The doctor advised us to consider removing her from the ventilator because she had "no viable brain wave activity." In other words, she was now supposedly "brain dead."

It was a difficult decision, and none of us wanted to remove her from the ventilator. But we were mostly in agreement that it should be done, especially if it was, in fact, true that there was no brain wave activity.

Most of us had already started grieving Mom's passing as the doctors told us there was no hope.

Then Aunt Jan visited Mom. Aunt Jan, with her loud, edgy voice, yelled at her, and all of a sudden, Mom opened her eyes.

Miraculously, Mom then began her difficult road to recovery, nearly eight months in hospital and in rehabilitation centers, before returning home. Given all the medications she was on while in the hospital, Mom told me later she didn't remember very much of that entire eight months.

Below is a short essay I wrote one day after helping take care of Mom.

In My Mother's Arms
(written in June of 2004)

Her hand, despite its age, is still smooth and remarkably free of brown spots. My own barely-weathered hand holds hers, and I am sitting next to her as she sleeps upright in a chair near her hospital bed. Her head leans on mine as she catches a short reprieve from the daily suffering she has had to endure.

As she nods off, I think about her life. I wonder what she was like as a playful child, then as a young bride in the 1950's, idealistic and ready to take on the world. Next, my mind wanders to the image of her standing next to my father's coffin, a widow at age 44, and how she consoled the four of us, her children, at the time young adults. I smile as I remember how she acted to be dating again, like a silly, giggling teenager, then to be a not-so-young bride and a not-so-young pregnant woman again. My eyes start to water as I think of her beaming face as she gazed down, with pride, on the crying face of her first grandchild.

After a few minutes, she wakes up and sits upright, then looks at me. "I'm glad you're here," she mouths the words she can't speak. "Me too," I whisper in her ear. Then her eyes glisten as she mouths, "I'm going to miss you when you're gone." "I know," I tell her, "I'm going to miss you too."

Now, my mother is crying, and I am trying desperately to control my own emotions. I know I must be strong for her. This is her fourth long month of being in a hospital, her fourth month of critical illness, of being on a respirator with a tube attached to her throat to assist her breathing. For her outgoing, independent, strong-willed personality, this is the last place that I thought she would be at the end of her life. But 47 years of smoking (she quit ten years ago), a long-term case of emphysema and a sudden, especially virulent case of pneumonia, forced this suffering on her.

She mouths something to me that I can't understand. I hand her the small pad she uses to write on, and she scribbles the words, "You don't mind spending a boring day with me?" As I see what she's writing, I blurt out, "Of course, I don't mind, Mom. I want to be here with you."

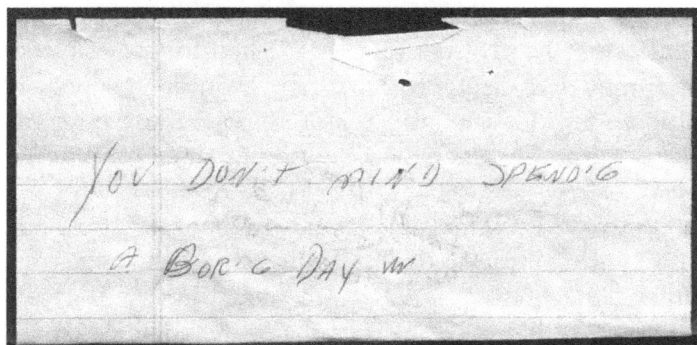

YOU DON'T MIND SPEND'G
A BOR'G DAY w/

She begins to cry again, something that she frequently does in this now-familiar environment. I think of how ironic it is that before all this happened, I could count on one hand the number of times I have seen her cry: when her mother died, when my father — her first husband — died, and the day after my wedding, when I was preparing to move far away from home. Now, crying is the norm for her, and I do my best not to cry, but to be strong for her.

It's hard for me to live far away when she's so critically ill. Although she's doing better and now breathing on her own for a good portion of the day, I find it difficult to stay connected to her. But I live in Canada, and I have a family to take care of, teenagers to parent, children to home school, a husband who needs me so I can only afford a week out of the month to spend time with her and help take care of her.

"You're doing so well, though, Mom," I tell her, hoping that it will help to make her feel better. She shakes her head, then mouths, "I feel lousy." I nod and then lean my head on her shoulder as we sit quietly amidst the noise of the machine pumping oxygen into her tracheostomy tube.

A short while later, she is moved back to her bed, and within minutes, she tells me, "I've messed myself." "That's okay," I tell her, "they will clean you up." "I hate it," she mouths to me. The nurse — a young, attractive African-American girl — comes in, and my mother asks her if I can stay. She nods and proceeds to clean my mother with tenderness and care. I hold my mom's hand as she starts to cry, the humiliation too difficult to bear at being washed by another. She tells me, "I feel like a burden." "Well, you're not," I say. "When you're loved, you're not a burden." The sweet nurse leans down and tells her, "You're not a burden, honey."

"You don't mind cleaning me up?" she asks her.

"I don't mind one bit," she replies. My mother's response was childlike: she held her arms out and pulled the young nurse down to kiss her on the cheek.

A few minutes later, my mother looks up at me and, with pleading eyes, asks, "Was I a good mother?"

Without hesitating, I reply, "Yes, Mom, you were a good mother." I pause, realizing I'm speaking in the past tense. "And you still are."

"I love you," she says to me. "And I love you too," I say, getting as close to her ear as I can. Before this illness, my mother, not normally an overly emotional person, would call me every morning and at the end of the call, would say, "I love you," to which I would respond, "Love you too, Mom." Those calls always helped me to stay connected to her, despite the distance that separated us.

"I miss our calls in the morning," I say to her. "Me, too," she says. Her hearing is dulled, and she's not able to speak audibly, so phone calls are limited to me calling her room and my sister or stepfather relaying the message to her.

"Pray with me," she says, and I begin saying an Our Father in her ear as she mouths the words along with me. Then I say a Hail Mary, and she mouths those words as well. Her breathing is labored now, and she closes her eyes.

"Hold me," she asks me, and I lay my head on her shoulder and place my arm around her, careful not to disturb the tubes leading to the machine. I remember as a young child, the feeling of being in her arms, safe from all the terrors of the world. Now, I hold her, allowing her to feel safe in the cold environment of the hospital.

As I embrace her, the woman who nurtured me, who once changed my diapers, who comforted me when I was afraid, I am overwhelmed by the irony of it all. And yet, despite her illness and fragility, she is still my mother, the woman who carried me in the loving safety of her womb for eight months, who took care of me for the first 20 years of my life.

Throughout these last four months, I often wonder why God spared her life. Her prognosis was poor, and, in the beginning, the doctors advised us to take her off the machine. But her will to live is strong, and she has always been a fighter. It is excruciating for us to watch her struggle to take every breath. After days like this one, days where I can tell my mother just how much I love her and appreciate all that she has done for me, I thank God that He has given us this time with her, these poignant moments where all we can think to say is "I love you."

As I continue to lay my head on her shoulder, she reaches her arm around me and holds me, and for a brief moment, I am that small child again, that daughter who is afraid, lost or alone, and I feel safe and secure in my mother's loving arms.

(End of essay.)

I visited at least once a month while she was recuperating. Joe was there all the time, so when I visited, I urged him to take a break. He would often go to the cafeteria for an hour or so, but he never missed a day in the eight months that she was in the hospital and rehabilitation center.
Remarkably, Mom rallied, and they eventually moved her into a rehab center in Philadelphia. She finally came home after eight months, and we were blessed to have her for three more years.

I don't think any of us took for granted those three additional years we had with Mom – especially Mom. Every time she talked to anyone, she always said, "I love you" before saying goodbye.

Later, when I spoke with her about her time in the hospital and rehabilitation center, she said she remembered little or nothing about either the hospital or rehab, probably because of the multiple drugs she was taking.

Her 70th birthday was rescheduled for the summer of 2005.

Celebrating Mom's 70th Birthday
L to R, back: Frank, Mom, Laurie, Mike
L to R, front: me, Diane

Grandmom with her grandchildren, Summer 2005
Back L to R: Josh, Ben, Mom, Timmy, Mandi
Front L to R: Thomas, Adam, Karli, Paul

Christmas 2006

In the weeks leading up to Christmas of 2006, I felt a strong desire to visit Mom. I don't know why, but I suspected that it would be her last Christmas. So I conspired with Joe and Laurie to plan a surprise visit that would start the day after Christmas. Of course, when we woke up that morning to leave, it was snowing...a lot. Since I was driving alone with my five sons (none of whom had their full driver's license yet), I wasn't going to travel in snow, so I waited. By noon, the snow had stopped, and we were ready to get on our way.

The trip was uneventful, and the weather improved. Around nine p.m., we pulled up to Mom's house. I knocked on the door, then opened it. Behind me, the boys all filed in. Mom was on the couch and hadn't yet looked up. Joe said, "Hi." Then Mom glanced up and did a double-take. She sat up. Then she started crying. We all hugged her, and she had to take the nose cannula out so she could blow her nose. But she couldn't stop crying. After that, she had a perpetual smile on her face the entire time we were there.

As usual, Mom and I shopped at Sam's, Acme, and J.C. Penney's. She couldn't walk from one end of the room to the other with her COPD, but she *could* drive. As long as she had her portable oxygen, she was fine.

Mom kept thanking me for surprising her and coming to visit. "What made you want to come this year?" she asked.

I hesitated, then she answered her own question: "This is probably my last Christmas."

"Now, you don't know that, Mom."

"No," she said, "but I've already had almost three more years since my time in the hospital."

As it turned out, it was last time some of my boys saw their grandmother before she died.

Christmas 2006

Chapter Eight
Terminal Diagnosis

In the spring of 2007, while James and I were chaperoning a group of high school students in Europe, I received a frantic email from Laurie (who was at our house watching our boys) that Mom had been rushed to the hospital and was not doing well. Eventually, I was able to speak with Mom (it cost me $150 to call her from Florence, Italy!), and she assured me that she was doing okay, and there was no need to rush home.

However, James and I arrived back home to the news that the doctors could do nothing more for Mom, and she was being sent home and put into hospice. When Frank brought her home, she said, "I'm coming home to die, aren't I?"

A hospital bed was brought in and set up in the living room, along with the oxygen machine.

During the next five months, I traveled down to New Jersey every two to three weeks with my three youngest boys (since I was still homeschooling). I helped take care of Mom, and we had many conversations about God, life, and heaven. I couldn't lift Mom up or help her off the toilet because she was a lot bigger/taller than I, but I could do just about everything else for her. She verbally walked me through making her recipes for roast beef, spaghetti sauce "gravy," and pork loin (some of which I've continued to use).

One day, when she was thanking me for doing something for her, I said, "You don't have to thank me, Mom. I just hope I can give back a small portion of what you gave to me for so many years. I mean, I can never repay you for my life, but I love being able to care for you." She cried. Until her viral pneumonia three years previous, I could count the number of times Mom had cried on one hand. As she neared the end of her life, she cried more frequently.

However, I will always remember those emotional conversations we had over the next several months.

"Do you think I'll get to see Jesus, El?"

Without hesitation, I said, "Absolutely, Mom. You believe in Him."

"But I haven't been the best person and haven't always gone to Mass."

"Well, no one is perfect, Mom. We're all sinners. As long as you're sorry, you'll see Jesus."

"You know, El, you've never given me one moment of grief." (I'm sure her memory was very selective at this point. For example, there was that time when I was doing cartwheels in the living room and knocked into her arm as she was entering from the kitchen. I'm quite sure Mom received a bad bruise on her arm from that incident. There was also the time when I was a teenager that I was crying because a TV program wasn't on and she told me to stop being a cry baby (in retrospect, I *was* crying for no good reason.)

Anyway, I decided not to remind her of those incidents. Then she said, "Really. I never lost a night's sleep from the time you were a baby right up to now."

I remember one particular conversation toward the end of her life when she said, "This is all my fault. I'm dying because I smoked for so many years, even after the doctor told me I should stop." She paused. "I hope God can forgive me," she said.

"He will forgive you because you're sorry. Now you have to forgive *yourself*."

She sighed. "You're right."

Mom's wit and sense of humor never left her, even that last summer of her life. We were chatting on the phone when she said, "Hey, El, I was just watching a show about the Little People of America. Did you know that the maximum height for that organization is four feet, ten inches? You're four feet, nine. You should join them."

"Um, okay. And why would I want to join Little People of America?"

"Then you can go to their conventions and feel like one of the tallest people in the room." She laughed.

On August 7, 2007, I was at home in Canada and planning my next trip down to New Jersey for the following week. I got a frantic call from Laurie saying that Mom was not doing well, and the hospice nurse said that I should come immediately.

I quickly packed bags for myself and my three youngest sons, and we started on the trek down to New Jersey. Of course, I waited for a long time at the border and finally made it to Cortland, New York, which is the halfway point from our house in Ontario to Mom's house in New Jersey. I called, and Laurie answered. When I told her that we were in Cortland, I could hear my Mom yelling, "She's only in Cortland? Tell her I love her and to be careful."

Those were her last words to me.

Laurie later told me that Mom had slipped into a coma shortly after that. When we arrived five hours later, my sister-in-law Karen took my two youngest boys, Adam and Paul – then ages eleven and eight) home with her while Tim stayed with us. When my stepfather and Tim went to bed, Laurie and I prayed the Litany of the Saints, which Mom had asked us to do when the time was close.

Laurie was a bit reluctant to say the Litany of the Saints at that point because, I think, she didn't want it to seem like we were giving up hope that Mom would pull out of the coma. I reassured her that one could say the Litany of the Saints at any time, for any person, and they didn't have to be dying. Of course, reciting that prayer for a dying person, I believe, can be powerful.

So we recited the Litany of the Saints, then we said the Divine Mercy Chaplet. I went upstairs to bed. Laurie didn't want to leave Mom alone, so she slept on the couch in the living room.

At about six a.m., I woke up and checked on Mom. Her breathing was labored, and her skin was starting to get cool; the oxygen machine continued to click and purr. Mom still had a weak pulse, though, so I whispered into her ear. "I love you so much, Mom. If you have to go, it's okay. We're all going to be fine. I'll see you again someday in heaven." I kissed her forehead and returned upstairs to pray for another hour or so.

By that time, family members started arriving to keep the bedside vigil with Mom. My siblings were all present, and I was sitting on the couch next to my brother, Frank. All of a sudden, I felt as if Mom was on the ceiling looking down at us. As I started to glance upward, my brother said, "It's weird, El, I feel like Mom is on the ceiling looking down at us."

Mom entered eternal life on the Feast of St. Dominic,

August 8, 2007.

The funeral Mass took place on the Feast of St. Maximilian Kolbe, August 14. It was beautiful. James sang Shubert's "Ave Maria," and his rendition was so moving that everyone sobbed. James said it was one of the hardest things he'd ever had to do because he couldn't cry while he was singing the song. Only at the cemetery did he finally let loose.   At the restaurant after the cemetery, I gave the eulogy. Afterward, my stepfather came up to me and said, "El, that was a perfect eulogy. Your mom would be very proud of you."

While many people might not believe in a supreme being or an afterlife, I will always be grateful that God allowed us the knowledge that Mom's soul was looking down on us and on her way to eternal life.

Grief counselors say you never get over a person's death; you just get through it. The pain is still there. I miss Mom very much. Losing a mother is difficult, no matter what age you are.

In the first few years after she died, there were many times that I would pick up the phone to tell Mom something exciting...and then I realized that she already knew.

Chapter Nine

Memories of Mom
From Others

Laurie (daughter):
Mom was always selfless when it came to her children. I started dancing when I was five, and she came faithfully to every dance recital. The recitals were typically in June, and the auditorium was not air-conditioned. Even when it was torturously hot, she was at every show. One year, she and a few of the other parents even chipped in to rent fans for the weekend.

She usually enjoyed the shows, especially the tap and ballet routines, but when I went to college, the only option on campus for dance classes was Modern dance. So, while she didn't quite appreciate that as much, she still drove over two hours each way to see me perform.

When I was home from college one summer, I wanted to hear a talk and see a performance by a modern dance choreographer taking place not far from my college. Even though the topic didn't really interest her, she drove me over two hours each way so I could attend. When we were driving back, we got concerned that we might be having car troubles because we heard what sounded like a flapping noise, like something was loose and flapping against the car. When we stopped at a rest area to check it out, I opened my door and realized that my skirt had been caught in the door and was flapping against the side of the car for most of the ride home. Fortunately for me, she found the humor in it.

She loved Christmas and everything about it. She had a Christmas Club at the bank to save for the holiday and started shopping months in advance. She would bake butter cookies, chocolate chip cookies with Toll House semi-sweet mini morsels and chopped walnuts and raspberry preserve cookies. We would watch 24 hours of *A Christmas Story* on Christmas Eve for almost 24 hours. She said it reminded her of her parents. Every year, I would be overwhelmed with gifts, even after I stopped believing in Santa Claus. As a young adult, she must have purchased an entirely new wardrobe for me every Christmas.

When she was near death, and we called my sister to come down from Canada, Mom knew I was talking on the phone with her and concerned about her safety while driving, said, "Tell her to be careful."

When she knew she was approaching death, she would tell people, "I just want to see Jesus."

Right before she died, the hospice nurse saw she was struggling to breathe and wanted to give her a medication to calm her. When she learned that this medication might sedate her and she wouldn't have another opportunity to speak to us, her last words were, "You were the best husband and kids that anyone could ask for. I love you."

Frank (son):
When Mom first got sick in '04, was comatose, and the nurse said she "probably won't wake up," she DID wake up and was in the rehab places for a long time - her appreciation of getting sort of a second chance to live longer was always evident. She always said "love you" to any of us at the end of any phone conversation, and she was just totally thankful and always appreciated whatever time she had left. I cannot remember any instance where she was mad or disgusted (there may have been, but I just don't remember any).

Also, during that time, Joe was the epitome of what devotion, dedication, and love are.

Karen (daughter-in-law):
Betti was the best mother-in-law ever.

Mike (son):
When our Mother asked me to get her a glass of water when I was a kid, I always gave her the water completely filled to the top of the glass! (I guess I did this because I was being a "wise guy"). I CONTINUED to do this as an adult, this time as a

joke—and it ALWAYS made our Mother smile, reminding her of all the times I did it as a child.

When Mom, Joe, Laurie, and I went out to dinner. She would always say to the waiter/waitress "thaaaank you veddie much."

Another memory I have is when Frank would harass me, for example: he would fart in my face, then I would do the same to him (I know, not very mature), HOWEVER, our mother would ALWAYS catch ME engaging in the retaliation, but she NEVER caught Frank, who would start it.

James (son-in-law):
After years of parenting, I can now fathom the inner trepidations of Mrs. Betti Power when she first met the Canadian boy for which her daughter, Ellen, might someday leave home...leave the country, in fact! Who was this introverted artist from the North, anyway? What totally impressed me was how she would diplomatically bring up topics when I was conversing with her, sometimes on a drive to the supermarket or the 'fruit stand', on a day when she needed assistance with the grocery shopping. She raised topics that would serve as subtle requests for me to show her who I was...who was taking her Ellen away. She had a sharp mind, a love of language, and could carry on one of these motherly probing conversations, all the while convincing me that we were just having a friendly chat. An amazing woman on so many levels...but this one blew me away.

Mandi Gable (granddaughter):
Grandmom gave me an appreciation for classical music because she always listened to it in the car. I also remember her swearing a lot, especially while driving.

One memory, in particular, stands out. I don't remember how old Laurie and I were, but it was after she quit smoking, and she was chewing gum. She had some dental work done before we were supposed to go to Wildwood. She was in a lot of pain, but she still went and wanted to go on the beach, despite all the pain she was in.

Ben Hrkach (grandson):
I love how Grandmom used to surprise us with visits to our home in Canada. Sometimes my brothers and I would be playing outside around four p.m., and a car would drive into our driveway. It would take us a few seconds, but we would then all realize that Grandmom was here for a visit! Other times, we'd be out for some reason, and then as we were driving back to our house, we'd see a car in our driveway and recognize Grandmom's car and come to the conclusion that she was here for a visit! I'd always try and guess when she might be coming up for a surprise visit, but she stumped me time and time again!

When we would go to her house in New Jersey for a week-long visit, I'll never forget how, when I'd get up in the morning, I'd walk to the den and see her typing away on her computer. She'd give me a big hug, ask how I was doing, and then I'd sit down and watch Cartoon Network for most of the morning.

I'll never forget her hospitality, her warmth, her humour, her generosity, and her love. It was always exciting when she came to visit us, and my family was also so excited to go and visit her.

Tim Hrkach (grandson):
I love how Grandmom used to surprise us and come up to Canada. Because I was bigger than my brothers (and had big hands), Grandmom told me I was "good, stvrong vorking stock," in an Eastern European accent.

Adam Hrkach: (grandson):
I remember when we surprised Grandmom the day after Christmas in 2006. When we came in, she cried, she was so happy. She cried so hard that she had to take that thing out of her nose to blow her nose. I was glad we made her so happy that she cried.

Janet Griffin (niece)
Aunt Betti's laughter was infectious. You couldn't help but be happy around her. She was charming and enchanting. I spent many summers at Uncle Frank and Aunt Betti's house. She got angry at me one time when I wrote a boy's name (my crush) on every surface in indelible ink. I also remember her

giving me a dollar to separate pages for her court transcripts, feeding liver to Chalkie and Tinker, and dancing to Abba.

Mary Eastman Vaccara (niece):

I will always remember her smile, her quick wit, and her laugh. And her big heart. Lots of love in her heart. I remember once when I was complaining about my mom in some way, and she gave me some very good advice: "Have patience and tolerance; don't judge too harshly; you don't really know what someone has been through."

Karen Eastman Stanley (niece):

I remember Aunt Betti crying when she heard of the JFK assassination. At the bus stop on Denfield Street on cold days, Aunt Betti wore a maxi coat and shielded Ellie under it. I remember driving to Ellie's baby shower in 1987 with Aunt Betti, Aunt Floss, Laurie, and Mandy, and I helped her drive when she was tired. A car would speed by me on the highway and she'd say, "What'd you do, Kar, park the car?" I recall how happy she was with Joe, and how thrilled she was to have grandkids! She had a great sense of humor. I remember her sliding down the splash waterslide she created for one of Laurie's parties. She made great birthday cakes and she'd add vanilla extract and other items to box cakes to create masterpieces.

Also, I recall Aunt Betti inviting me to stay overnight with Diane in Denfield Street, and I had this awful cough, and Aunt Betti got up in the middle of the night to give me cough medicine – I guess I was keeping everyone awake.

I remember staying overnight with Diane on Carlisle Street in Philadelphia, and Diane and I took a huge, bubble bath and gabbed for a long time until Aunt Betti got upset because tub overflowed and spilled into the downstairs living room!

Jean Decky (friend)

My friendship with your mother started almost from the first day my son Brian began school at St. Teresa's. I was looking to do some volunteer work at the school, and I approached Sister Joseph to see if there was something I could do. She introduced me to your mom, and from then on, I had plenty to do! Your mother took me under her wing and introduced me to the "lunch moms." It was the lunch program your mother ran three days a week. Wednesdays were hotdogs that were made and wrapped all morning in the kitchen, Thursdays were hoagies that we picked up at the deli or meatball sandwiches that her friend Elena made, and Friday was pizza day. We asked one grade each week to send in snacks on Friday. All the lunches were then delivered to the classrooms. Your mom was there every day to oversee everything. She was also there on Mondays when the lunch orders were collected for the week, and the money counted. She printed up the order sheets and delivered them on Friday to be brought back in on Monday.

She spent so much time doing everything she could to make money for the school and, more importantly, to give the kids a great school experience. Like putting together an Easter basket or a Christmas Stocking filled with goodies to be chanced off. All of this came out of her own pocket, which she never wanted anyone to know about. I think she knew every one of their names and not just the kids in Laurie's class. She knew them all.

She enjoyed working at the Christmas Bazaar at the Home and School table. She was there for the Summer Lawn Festival, helping out wherever they needed her from the food prep in the mornings to the food booth at night. She helped to organize field day for the kids every year (more hotdogs and chips!) and ice pops.

All of this she did while holding down a busy and important job and getting Laurie to dance class or wherever she needed to be.

I know you already know this, but her kids and grandkids were the loves of her life. She was so proud of every one of you. I think that's where she got all her energy. There wasn't anything she wouldn't do to support each and every one of you.

November of 2005, Ben and Mom

Which brings us to November of '05. We came up to see Ben play Pilate in *Jesus Christ Superstar*. Your mom and I were staying at the motel, and we went to bed. All of a sudden, in the middle of the night, her oxygen machine set off an alarm, which woke me up and scared the heck out of me. I yelled, "Bet, Bet!" No answer. Then I was in a panic. Finally, she woke up and I asked her, "are you okay? Your machine is going off!" She said, "Oh yeah, I'm fine. It just does that sometimes," then she went back to sleep. Needless to say, I spent the rest of the night with one eye open!

The drive home from Canada was scary because as we were getting into the Conshohocken area, her oxygen tanks were running out. I think you guys were behind us. Traffic was pretty heavy, and it seemed like it took us forever to get home. But all's well that ends well, and I know that the trip was so worth it for her to see all her grandsons.

I remember the trips to Wildwood Crest, which she always seemed to enjoy.

We spent hours and hours talking on the phone, and we could do that every day. I don't know how we had that much to talk about, but we did. We shared so much. The good and the bad. Stuff we would never share with anyone else. She was my best friend, and I miss not having someone to tell my troubles to or really share my joys with. She had a heart of gold, a great sense of humor, and what you saw was what you got. My final memory was the last day I saw her. As I was almost out the door, she hollered behind me, "Love you, girl," and I answered, "Love you too, Bet."

I have her little bowling pin from 91-92 Rainbow League season sitting on my desk. It has her name and her '215' high game on it. There are other little things around my house that remind me of her, things we picked out for the Christmas Kit or something Irish she gave me. Sometimes I say one of her little sayings and then say, "Right, Bet?"

Appendix

Mom's Sayings

Stick with me and I'll have you farting through silk.

That's no ladle, that's my (wife) (knife)

Blow it out your ass

One 'Aw Shit' wipes out ten 'Atta Boys'

He thought he farted but he really shit himself

Shit and two is eight

I feel like a half-sucked sour ball

Who's she, the cat's mother? (She never liked being referred to as "she.")

Tote that bar, lift that bale, get a little drunk and you'll land in jail

Chevrolet Bouquet Bon Ami (when asked if she spoke French)

My mom cooks corn and peas in the same pot (pees in the same pot)

Your breath would knock a buzzard off a shit wagon

Think it'll hurt the rhubarb? Not if it's in the can

God willing and the Creek don't rise

Ass over tin cups

Is the pope Catholic?

You're big and ugly enough to do it yourself

If we asked her where something was (like a book or one of our toys), she'd pull the bottom of her eye down and say, "Right here filed under B," or whatever the first letter of what we were looking for was.

When it was cold out, she'd say, it's colder "than a witch's tit."

If she was typing at her desk and wanted a drink of water, she would say, "Hey, El, can you get me a dinka wawa."

If someone passed gas (or if she did) and it was particularly stinky, she'd say, "It smells like something crawled inside of you and died." (Her mom evidently said this too!)

If someone passed gas audibly, she'd say, "that's a low flying mallard," or "did someone step on a duck?"

If she happened to borrow money from us kids (when we were teens), when we bothered her to pay it back, she'd tease us and say, "Put a price on your life and then subtract that amount." But she always paid us back.

If we said that our clothes didn't look good or our face had broken out, she'd say, "No one's going to notice driving down the street at 50 miles per hour."

Mom's Favorite Movies

Titanic (1997)
After seeing this in theaters, Mom couldn't get enough of this movie and the incredible special effects. She watched the DVD of this every few months.

West Side Story
A modern *Romeo and Juliet* story, Mom saw this in theaters, then took me at least once to see this in the theater when it was re-released in the late 60's.

Psycho

Uncle John had seen this movie but would only tell Mom it was the scariest movie he'd ever seen. He just kept saying, "Go see it." She and Aunt Jan finally went to see it. After that, she didn't want to take a shower for months.

My Cousin Vinny

Mom loved Joe Pesci and laughed every time she saw this movie about an inexperienced lawyer who ends up defending his cousin.

Ed and His Dead Mother

Mom's tastes in movies were varied. This is a movie about Ed (Steve Buscemi), whose mother has been dead for a year. A guy appears at his door, claiming he can reanimate his mother for $1000. But all doesn't go as smoothly as Ed wants. When I watched this with Mom, she laughed hysterically throughout the movie.

A Christmas Story

This was Mom's favorite Christmas movie because it reminded her of her parents and her childhood. Of course, she also enjoyed the quirky humor of the movie as well and would watch the movie over and over again when there was a holiday marathon going on.

Mom's Favorite TV Shows
Magnum PI (she loved Tom Selleck)
All in the Family
Dragnet and Adam-12

Law and Order
CSI
The Price is Right

Eulogy for Betti Power
August 14, 2007
Given by Ellen Gable Hrkach

Wife, mother, sister, grandmother, mother-in-law, stepmother, sister-in-law, aunt, cousin, friend.

She was Betti (with an i)

To us, she was simply "Mom."

She was witty, loving, generous, giving, unselfish.

She enjoyed her grandchildren, transcribing (and was the fastest typist I know). She loved surprising people, visiting Canada, talking on the phone, crossword puzzles, reading. Her favorite music was *West Side Story*, *Jesus Christ Superstar*, Abba, and Fleetwood Mac. When I was a child, I remember her blaring the soundtrack of *West Side Story* on the stereo whenever she did her spring cleaning or Christmas cleaning.

Upon meeting Mom, most people immediately felt comfortable with her, and she would often strike up a conversation at the grocery store with people she didn't know.

She cherished having a new baby in her late 40's and all that came with it: being a lunch mother, taking Laurie to dance lessons, and Catholic school.

She loved Christmas shopping and would begin her shopping in July and finish before November.

She enjoyed watching television, and her favorite shows were the Sopranos, Law and Order, Price is Right, ER, Magnum PI, and All in the Family. One of her favorite movies was "Titanic." and she would watch the DVD every few months.

She used some unique sayings: "God willing and the Creek don't rise." When asked if she could speak French, she would reply, "Sure, I can. Chevrolet, bouquet, Bon Ami." When one of her kids was misbehaving (usually Frank), she would say, "I'm gonna drop kick you across Center Avenue." Whenever I stood next to her, she would always say, "El, are you standing in a hole?" If we referred to her as "she" and not "Mom," she would say, "Who's she, the cat's mother?" Whenever anyone asked how she was doing, she would reply, "Well, I'm still on this side of the grass, so I guess I'm doing fine."

Mom described herself as an "independent," but has only voted Republican twice.

Whenever someone in the hospital or at home would ask if they could get her anything, she would always reply, "Tom Selleck."

When asked what the most memorable days of her life were, she replied, "My wedding days and the days I gave birth to my five children."

Mom was a fighter, not necessarily aggressive. Still, she's survived some pretty challenging experiences: her husband (my father's) nervous breakdown while she was in labor with my youngest brother, Frank;

kidney failure in the '60s, which led to the removal of one of her kidneys, which caused her to drop to 80 pounds (at five foot six, made her a walking skeleton); becoming a widow at 44; then having to deal with COPD and emphysema over the last ten or so years. When she first became critically ill in 2004, the doctors told us there was no hope for her, to take her off of life support. Instead, she eventually woke up. She finally came home after eight months of hospitalization to the new normal: oxygen machine, nebulizer treatments, myriad pills, and medications. Although it's been an uphill battle, she has had a strong will to live.

This past March, when James and I were in Europe, she became critically ill again, but she told my sister, Laurie, not to tell me that she was sick again because she didn't want me to worry.

However, Laurie doesn't lie. When I found out that my mom was doing poorly, I called her hospital room (from Italy), and although the call cost me a lot of money, but it was well worth it to hear her voice.

Finally, in April, the doctors told Mom that there wasn't much more that could be done for her because her lungs were so damaged and that she was being sent home on hospice care. When arriving home, she said to my brother, Frank, "I'm coming home to die, right?"

Whenever any of us helped to take care of her, she always thanked us profusely, whether it was for emptying her commode chair, making her breakfast or dinner, or a snack of a soft pretzel or an ice cream cone. She often apologized for being a burden. I told her that it was a joy to help take care of her, to give back to her just a small portion of what she had given to me, and I know my stepfather and my siblings all feel the same.

Mom, we miss you. *Requiescat in pace.*

Mom's Family Tree

(6) John F. May
1896-1969

(4) Frank Gable
1928-1978

Mike 1956

(1) Diane 1956-2019

(5) **Elizabeth (Betti) May**
1934-2007

(5) Ellen 1959

(2) Flossie 1917-1988
(7) Jack 1927-1997
(4) Ed 1929-1994
(4) Janet 1937

(2) Frank 1961

(6) Joseph Power
1933-2012

(6) Elizabeth (Bessie)
Gillespie
1898-1967

Laurie 1981

(number) denotes number of children, including stillborns

147

Mom's Recipes

Christmas Raspberry Preserve Cookies

One-pound butter or margarine
4 cups of white flour
1/2 cup walnuts (for allergies, omit)
1.5 to 2 cups of brown sugar
2 teaspoons of cloves
2 teaspoons of cinnamon
2 teaspoons of baking powder
3 eggs, beaten
one jar raspberry preserves or jam (seedless)

Mixing by hand, mix butter/margarine, flour, cloves, cinnamon, baking powder until it resembles fine meal. Add eggs, 1/4 c. walnuts and brown sugar. Mix well. Split into two parts and refrigerate for a few hours. After refrigeration, roll out dough on two clean sheets of wax paper, add the rolled-out dough to the bottom of a large cookie sheet with a 1/4 lip around. Spread raspberry jam evenly. Roll out other part of dough on two clean sheets of waxed paper and carefully lay on top of dough and raspberry jam. Sprinkle with rest of walnuts and cook at 350 degrees for 35-40 minutes (until edges are brown).

Cool completely, then cut into squares.

New Year's Vegetable Soup

Mom's grandparents and parents made this soup every New Year's Day, and I have continued this tradition. Mom often made this on New Year's Eve, then put the entire soup pot outside to cool, and heated it up on New Year's Day while we were all watching the Mummers Parade on television.
(Warning: this makes A LOT of soup. Be prepared to give a lot away or freeze.)

One large beef soup bone
one can (medium) tomato paste
water
half head of cabbage, chopped in small pieces
four white potatoes, chopped
one onion, chopped
one medium bag of frozen peas
four celery stalks chopped
two sweet potatoes, chopped
one turnip/rutabaga, chopped (slightly cook first for ease in chopping)
four carrots, chopped
one medium size bag of frozen green beans, chopped
one medium size bag of frozen corn (the recipe calls for shoe peg corn, but we don't have this in Canada)
one package frozen or fresh okra, chopped
one can or frozen package of lima beans (I leave these out since I don't like lima beans)
Using a large soup pot, add beef bone, fill with water to about 2/3 full, add tomato paste and stir until mixed.
Add all ingredients and cook on medium heat for five to eight hours or until frothy and vegetables are tender.

Chocolate Chip Cake

Batter
1 stick (1/2 c) of butter or margarine
2 c flour
1 c sugar
2 eggs
1 tsp vanilla
1 tsp baking powder
1 tsp baking soda
1 c sour cream
1/2 package chocolate chips

Mix 1/2 chopped walnuts
1/4 c sugar
2 tsp cinnamon

Batter: cream butter, sugar, eggs, vanilla. Mix dry ingredients separately. Alternately add dry ingredients and sour cream until mixed well. Add chocolate chips.

Put half of the batter in a greased and floured tube pan, sprinkle half of mix, then put other half of batter over that and sprinkle rest of mix.

Bake at 350 F for 45 minutes or until done.

Acknowledgments

Special thanks to my sister, Laurie, and to my brothers, Mike and Frank, for reading early copies of this book and sharing their own stories or adding details to my stories. Also thanks to Frank to sending me some of the photos I used in this book.

Special thanks to my husband, James, for helping with the cover design.

Thank you to everyone who shared stories about Mom.

A posthumous thank you to Aunt Flossie (1917-1988), Uncle John (1909-2005), and Aunt Peggy (1937-2003), who all helped Mom during those difficult months when my father was in Ancora and after my brother Frank was born. Aunt Floss and Uncle John were also a huge help to my father when Mom was in the hospital for five weeks in 1967. Finally, my gratitude to Aunt Floss and Uncle John for their tremendous financial assistance to our family as I was growing up.

A special posthumous thank you to the best stepfather ever (and first cousin once removed), Joe (1933-2012), who took excellent care of Mom in her last few years and never once complained.

About the Author

Ellen Gable (Hrkach) is an award-winning author (2010 IPPY Gold medal, 2015 IAN finalist, 2019 IAN finalist), publisher (2016 CALA), editor, self-publishing book coach, speaker, NFP teacher, Marriage Preparation Instructor, Theology of the Body teacher, and past president of the Catholic Writers Guild. She has written eleven books and is a contributor to numerous others. Her novels have been collectively downloaded over 700,000 times on Kindle, and her books have nearly three-quarters of a million pages read on KDP. Five of her novels have been translated into Portuguese, Italian, Spanish, French, and Greek. Four of her books are available on Audible as audiobooks. The author and her husband, James, are the proud parents of five adult sons, seven precious souls in heaven, and are the devoted grandparents to one adorable grandson. In her spare time, Ellen enjoys reading on her Kindle, researching her family tree, and watching live-stream classic movies and TV shows. Her website is ellengable.com.

Follow Ellen:
Twitter: @ellengable
Facebook: facebook.com/ellengable
Pinterest: @ellengable
Instagram: @ellengable

www.ingramcontent.com/pod-product-compliance
Lightning Source LLC
Chambersburg PA
CBHW032134040426
42449CB00005B/234